YORKSHIRE'S
HISTORIC
PUBS

PETER THOMAS

SUTTON PUBLISHING

Sutton Publishing Limited
Phoenix Mill · Thrupp · Stroud
Gloucestershire · GL5 2BU

First published 2005

Copyright © Peter Thomas, 2005

Title page photograph: The pub sign for The
Vine on the Headrow, Leeds.

British Library Cataloguing in Publication Data
A catalogue record for this book is available from the
British Library.

ISBN 0-7509-3983-4

Typeset in 10.5/13.5 Photina.
Typesetting and origination by
Sutton Publishing Limited.
Printed and bound in England by
J.H. Haynes & Co. Ltd, Sparkford.

Lupton and Mrs Whitelock with the car from which he lost his flute (see pages 74–7). It was
he who transformed the pub into what we see today. (*Photograph courtesy of Sarah Whitelock*)

CONTENTS

The impressive fireplace at the Bingley Arms, Bardsey.

The Chequers at Bilton in Ainsty; one of the examples of the sign believed to have originated in Roman times.

INTRODUCTION

Nothing is more English than the village pub, except perhaps a game of cricket. To have the pub facing the cricket field is sheer heaven, although if its wall provides the players with a boundary, 'regulars' would do well to park their cars out of the line of fire if damage and harsh words are to be avoided.

Tradition, or a handing down of customs from generation to generation, is strong and deep in this country. The tradition of a seat under the trees watching cricket with a glass of beer is far more, though, than a sentimental picture of continuing village life. Pubs have provided atmosphere, hospitality and fellowship for many hundreds of years; today's meat and potato pie or fish and chips may be traditional, but that menu goes back a very short time compared with the days of the first drinking houses.

In the earliest days brewing was a domestic activity, mainly carried out by women, or 'brewsters'. Local applications at 'brewster' sessions for the granting of licences in the twenty-first century recall this early custom of the brewing and selling of ale.

Of course, some brewsters' products were more popular than others, attracting more customers to their homes where villagers could meet, drink and socialise. From this came the 'public' house as we know it, at a pub which is also a home, with the publican as a host and the customer a guest.

The brewing of ale from barley had been going on for centuries before the Romans came in 55 BC, but the brew did not develop into beer containing hops until after 1400, when the first hopped version arrived in England from Flanders. Gradually, as its popularity grew, the 'new' beer was brewed more widely and hops were being grown in England for beer production. Today the terms 'ale' and 'beer' mean much the same, although strictly speaking ale is a brew containing just a small trace of hops.

We have good evidence to suggest that when the Romans came they established drinking places in their settlements and particularly on their military roads, which were both long and hard. These *tabernae* (from which our 'tavern' comes) must have been a very welcome sight; they identified themselves with a bush in the form of a bundle of vine leaves hanging outside. Wine was a universal drink, although ale was also usually on sale.

As well as the bush outside, travellers might see the 'chequers' sign on a board or wall, which showed that games like draughts could be played there. It is a commonly used sign today; in Yorkshire we have it for example at Bilton in Ainsty near Wetherby and at Ledsham just north of Castleford. Bush and vine are both hard to find, although the vine sign can be seen on the Headrow in Leeds. Rare too is a painted bunch of grapes kept on display over the front wall of a pub; look for it on the front of the King's Head in the Market Place at Richmond.

Roman *tabernae* on military roads must have served quite small numbers of travellers, but in later centuries, as the movement of people began to increase, the need for places for rest and refreshment became more and more important and encouraged the setting up of inns for those on the roads. Places of pilgrimage such as Canterbury attracted large numbers of pilgrims who needed rest on the way; it became a profitable business for the monasteries ready and able to open inns for those on pilgrim routes or on Church business.

One of Yorkshire's fascinating examples is the Bingley Arms at Bardsey near Leeds. Mentioned in Domesday Book, it was known as the Priests' Inn from AD 953 until 1780, when it was renamed. The inn was connected with Kirkstall Abbey and offered rest and hospitality for monks travelling to St Mary's at York. A priest's hole in the chimney is on view, an exciting glimpse of the past life of the building. We even know the name of the brewer here in 953: one Samson Ellis.

The growth of trading centres and markets brought drovers and merchants across the country and even from overseas. To meet the growing need of wayfarers on foot or on horseback, inns in market places and out in the countryside grew in number and quality. Large country estates also provided places of refreshment for their workers whose earnings often included ale; many village pubs today recall this with their signs showing the arms of the lord of the manor or important landowner, such as the Yorke Arms at Ramsgill in Nidderdale, now advertising itself as a restaurant with rooms.

The Kings Head in the Market Place at Richmond with the bunch of grapes above the main entrance.

But of all the influences on the development of pubs, the most outstanding was the introduction of coach services: from 1657 onwards the growth of such travel was enormous, encouraged by the establishment of turnpike trusts that improved roads and charged vehicles for their use. Coaching inns not only had to provide food and accommodation for passengers, but in addition needed to organise stabling for horses, which had to be changed about every 15 miles. All the activity would have taken place in a courtyard, access being through an archway alongside the inn. This pattern becomes quite familiar on important routes such as the Great North Road, where the Golden Lion at Northallerton was a well-known stage. After Thirsk it was the next stop northwards, serving both private coach services and the mails. More remote routes needed stage stops too, and these inns became popular as a result; an example is the King's Arms at Askrigg in Wensleydale. It served as a coaching inn on the Richmond to Lancaster run and more recently played as the Drovers' Arms in *All Creatures Great and Small.*

The golden age of the coaching inn inevitably came to an end with the development of the railways, but it was not to be too long before car travel opened up new opportunities for well-managed country pubs, while town pubs also changed to meet changing social needs. Eating out has become increasingly popular and menus show the influence of foreign travel. The power of the large breweries has meant the loss of independence of many pubs and the closure of some, unable to cope with competition and rising costs. No doubt the extension of licensing hours has played a part in this and has added pressure on landlords.

Pub signs and their meanings

Going back to the Middle Ages and beyond, few people could read or write and had to depend on sign language in many ways for even their most basic needs. Shopping was a good example: signs were necessary to tell the public what a shop had for sale and streets in towns were lined with symbols of various kinds. Visit Half Moon Court at York Castle Museum to see some of these. The barber's pole has survived in many places and occasionally one still sees a so-called American Red Indian standing outside a tobacconist's shop.

While the bush, or bundle of vine leaves hanging outside, identified drinking places in this country in Roman times this did nothing to meet later needs when travel developed and the number of ale houses or pubs began to increase. It became important for publicans to be able to distinguish their houses from those of competitors by a prominent sign easily recognised by everyone, the more colourful and eye catching the better. Some signs became 'standards', like the Red Lion and the Rose & Crown; many have fascinating connections or origins. Some have become landmarks and are listed as bus stops.

The majority of signs are painted on hanging boards or are fixed to the front wall; much skill and imagination are required on the part of sign painters to capture the spirit of the chosen name of the pub. There are many framed in decorated wrought

The Old Starre Inne at Stonegate.

iron; the most extravagant of these is at the Three Swans at Market Harborough in Leicestershire.

Spectacular, but all too rare examples are the strangely named 'gallows' signs that extended right across the whole road. Their drawback was the danger they created for passers by; eventually the law forbade new ones from being erected. One timber arch that stood the test of time for many years crossed the A140 Norwich road at Stonham in Suffolk outside the Magpie. The bird stood on the centre of the cross bar, but in recent years it was wrecked by a large goods vehicle. After a long delay and much bureaucratic discussion its restoration was agreed and tradition triumphed; it looks magnificent again. York has a famous and handsome version in Stonegate at Ye Olde Starre Inne. A glimpse of York Minster can be detected in the distance.

1. YORKSHIRE'S HISTORIC PUBS

Where can you find a pub that overlooks a medieval battlefield, or keeps a flood marker in the bar, or takes its name from a famous racehorse? Read on and you will find them among the collection of Yorkshire's historic pubs in this book.

The variety of locations, from remote Ribblesdale to city centre Ripon, from the coast at Staithes to industrial Spen valley, is matched by a huge difference in the age and style of pub buildings. The licensees (more often landladies than in the past) and their regulars – all have a story of some kind to tell.

Food has been a revelation: from cordon bleu to the spectacular! The good old standards are there: fish, chips and peas and Yorkshire pudding and gravy. It would be an exaggeration to say that there are as many different recipes for meat and potato pie as there are pubs, but the variety is enormous. Pressed to say which dishes have been the most memorable, one has to confess carrot and coriander soup with Cheddar twist, and chips topped with melted cheese and bacon. Inventive, tasty and filling, both of them.

The only possible answer to the question how were the pubs in the book chosen? is good friends and sheer luck. Yorkshire pubs reflect the rich and multi-faceted county in which we live and should appeal to readers from Yorkshire – and, we hope, anywhere. If there is any single conclusion that can be drawn from the whole experience embraced by the pages that follow, it is the considerable number of pubs that have not appeared here and deserve to do so.

The door to Whitelocks, Leeds.

ALDBOROUGH: *SHIP INN*

Aldborough: A1M to J48 then follow signs to Boroughbridge. From St James' Square take the Aldborough road.

Aldborough owes its existence to the Romans, who founded a settlement here close to a crossing of the river Ure. Called *Isurium Brigantium*, it was linked by Roman roads to York and Hadrian's Wall; it became so important as a centre of government that it was pre-eminent in Yorkshire.

But why the Ship? Far from the sea here, of course, but possibly the pub took its name from the Ure crossing and the historic importance of river traffic. The licensees point to the extensive use of ships' timbers in the pub, particularly in and around the bar, as influencing the choice of name.

Standing across the road from St Andrew's Church, the pub may, in its earliest days, have been a house of shelter for travellers, but there is no positive evidence of this and the Ship is only one of many pubs in England close to the parish church. It is more likely that the first building on the site was a farmhouse, believed to date from 1392. In those days the farm was probably a beer house as well; the first use of the name Ship seems to have been in the sixteenth or seventeenth century. Many farms were also beer houses and had a brewery of sorts for their business use.

In the early nineteenth century two cottages stood by the roadside close to the Ship, separated from the pub by a narrow cart entry. Ducks and chickens wandered around freely. A sale notice in May 1870 described the Ship as an inn or public

The Ship Inn, Aldborough.

The beamed bar at the Ship.

house with brewhouse, wash house, cart sheds, stables and garden. Also listed were the two cottages with stables, piggery and excellent garden. Some time after this sale the cottages were demolished, allowing the Ship to use the land, which is now the car park.

The front of the Ship has two bay windows; these and its hanging sign would make the pub visible in Low Road among the dwellings close by. A glazed vestibule forms an entrance in the corner of the L-shaped building with a further doorway made of very old timbers leading to the bar. Tables in the dining area by the roadside windows are popular and there is a thirty-seat restaurant in the rear of the pub. A nautical atmosphere has been maintained: a ship's wheel is on the wall of the dining area and prints of ships as well as views of the Ship, past and present, are in the restaurant.

Aldborough is heavy with history and the Ship is well placed as a base for overnight visitors as well as those making day trips. Traces of the town's Roman walls are to be seen in a number of places and the museum has a fine collection of Roman pottery and coins. The parish church is believed to have been built on the site of a former Roman temple. Just beyond at the road junction is a tall monument commemorating the Battle of Boroughbridge in 1322 when King Edward II defeated the Earl of Lancaster; it was moved to its present position in the nineteenth century.

No visitor to Aldborough should miss the interest of a short walk to the green with its massive maypole. Around the green are some of the handsomest cottages to be seen in Yorkshire and at the top is the Old Court House with a plaque recording its history; until 1832 MPs were elected here for what was then a so-called rotten

Old Court House, Aldborough. Note the steps to the upper floor and the memorial.

borough. Below the plaque is a blue and white memorial to the crew of a Lancaster bomber who died in 1944 in a crash nearby that, but for their efforts, could well have been on Aldborough itself.

It is astonishing that this small peaceful place should have figured in a period that spanned the arrival of the Romans in the second century and the Second World War in the twentieth.

BAINBRIDGE: *ROSE & CROWN HOTEL*

Bainbridge: A1M north to Leeming Bar then A684 west via Leyburn.

From Semerwater the Bain, reputedly England's shortest river, flows into Bainbridge, one of the most attractive villages in the Dales. The massive green, bordered by trees, is overlooked by the fifteenth-century Rose & Crown, with the fells behind. Once the site of a Roman fort on Brough Hill, Virosidum controlled a road east to Aldborough and Boroughbridge in Yorkshire. Westward a road connected with the fort at Ribchester on the river Ribble in Lancashire.

There are few local customs that have been observed 'from time immemorial', but this was true in the case of the Bainbridge Forest Horn. Until recent years three blasts of the horn were blown at nine o'clock every night 'from Holyrood to Shrovetide'. The horn was blown on the green to guide back to shelter travellers lost in the forest of Wensleydale. There is now no forest, of course, and no one is likely to

The Rose & Crown, Bainbridge.

be lost on the modern signposted roads of the Dale, but for generations Bainbridge folk could set their clocks by the horn.

Sadly the custom has now ceased, but the last horn used is on display at the reception area in the Rose & Crown. There were earlier horns that have been lost and a very old one, said to be the original, is at Bolton Castle. The horn at the Rose & Crown is of buffalo horn and was brought into use in 1864. The hornblower of Bainbridge was traditionally a member of the Metcalfe family who were powerful and whose ancestral home was Nappa Hall. Now a farmhouse, it was fortified as a protection against Scottish raiders.

If you are looking for legend, this is where you will find it. The most famous story about Semerwater tells how a beggar arrived on the shore asking for food and water. The beggar was really an angel and the only kindness shown him came from an elderly couple. By the next day everyone except the couple had been drowned in the lake. Remains of a 3,000-year-old settlement have been found, no doubt giving rise to a legend relating to some distant tragedy. Since then generations of story telling and common belief have ensured its survival.

BECK HOLE: *BIRCH HALL INN*

Beck Hole: A169 Pickering–Whitby road. After Saltersgate fork left for Beck Hole.

Beck Hole is one of the unlikeliest candidates in Yorkshire to be included in a list of industrial villages – so tiny that it hardly qualifies as a village at all.

Birch Hall Inn stands close to the 1873 stone bridge over the Eller Beck, and whether going in the direction of Goathland or Whitby the visitor is faced by a strenuous and challenging climb uphill. On the Whitby side of the bridge is the green with its quoits pitches and most of the dwellings, while the Birch Hall and its neighbours are on the Goathland side.

No doubt in idyllic days, when time mattered less, travellers would have stopped for rest and refreshment here, but it was not until the nineteenth century that Birch Hall opened officially as a pub, serving also as a village store and occupying two stone cottages. These are conspicuously white next to the extension built by the landlord for some of the families who in the middle of the century arrived to work in the quarries, newly opened ironstone mines and smelting furnaces. The pub today has two small bars (although one is called the 'Big Bar') with flagged floors. Above the pub and shop two tenements remain with bedrooms reached by a wooden passageway.

The building of a railway to serve Beck Hole's industry and to link Whitby with the south brought even more workers, but by the 1870s the village's brief 'industrial

Birch Hall Inn, Beck Hole.

The interior of Birch Hall Inn.

revolution' was over. Soon evidence of it all began to disappear as buildings were demolished and their stone was put to other uses. The workers left to seek employment elsewhere and village life became peaceful once more.

Beck Hole once had its own station on George Stephenson's railway line between Whitby and Pickering, but a steep incline brought about a serious accident and a re-routing in 1865 closed Beck Hole's station. Today the North York Moors Railway between Pickering and Grosmont still gives passengers spectacular views of the Esk Valley and Newton Dale.

Licensees must enjoy Birch Hall and Beck Hole; certainly they seem reluctant to move. Perhaps the record is held by Mrs E.M. Schofield who was there for fifty-three years from girlhood to retirement. She is credited with putting up a notice behind the bar that offered 'Ale tomorrow for nothing'.

BEVERLEY: *WHITE HORSE INN (NELLIE'S)*

Beverley: M62 and A63 to the Humber Bridge, then A164 north.

Nellie's stands in Hengate, opposite St Mary's Church, with buses squeezing past down a narrow one-way system towards the bus station. So close is it to St Mary's that the land was probably originally church property and an inn here could have served the builders of churches in the town. Close to the Saturday Market, it must always have shared with several other pubs in the area the business that a market would bring.

The White Horse Inn, Beverley.

The historic interior of Nellie's.

Sketch of the bar by P. Kitchen.

The Saturday Market had been established by the twelfth century; by this time Beverley had become a commercial centre and exported woollen cloth across the North Sea. The market's importance led to the growth of the town, particularly in the market area, so it is not surprising to find such a fine church as St Mary's there. Close to the church are the handsome Memorial Gardens; Hengate reflects the development of Beverley into a social centre with attractive houses mainly from the eighteenth and nineteenth centuries.

Nellie's is earlier, from the seventeenth century, timber framed and brick fronted, differing from its neighbours by the elegant White Horse across and above the door. Inside, nothing seems to have changed for generations and it is claimed to be the best example of an unaltered nineteenth-century interior in the country. The main bar has a haphazard cluster of small rooms and narrow passages around it; all have boarded floors, plain wooden tables and other old furniture. Open fires and gas provide heating and lighting.

In spite of everything, perhaps *because* of everything, including the food, Nellie's has a considerable and loyal following. It is evident that atmosphere is all-important and here socialising goes on as it has always done in successful pubs over the centuries. Apart from the regulars, everyone asks 'Why Nellie's?' Nellie was the daughter of a tenant, Francis Collinson, who bought the pub in 1928. Following her father, she became landlady until 1976, gaining such a reputation that her name became universally used rather than the one above the door.

BEVERLEY: *BEVERLEY ARMS*

Beverley: From Hull (Humber Bridge) A164 north.

Before 1794 there was no pub called the Beverley Arms, as earlier than that date it was known as the Blue Bell. Old records show that as far back as 1686 there was a Bell Inn at Beverley and this may well have been the Blue Bell.

Although information on the Blue Bell and the early years of the Beverley Arms is sketchy it seems that the Blue Bell had a sign of the 'gallows' type, using posts and a bar to carry the sign over all or part of the road. Few of these remain today; in Yorkshire Ye Olde Starre Inne at York is a survivor. The present hanging sign of the Beverley Arms is more conventional; its pillared entrance and elegant rooms suggest a definite move up-market away from the status of a posting and coaching inn of 200 years ago to that of a first class hotel today.

As an inn serving numbers of eighteenth-century road travellers there would have been the customary courtyard with space for stables, coaches and possibly a brewhouse. The eighteenth-century version of 'fast food' would have been served as changes of coach horses took place.

The coming of the railways changed all this and in common with other hotels in Yorkshire market towns the Beverley Arms needed to provide its own transport to and from the railway station. The development of car travel and tourism brought other changes, including a new kind of visitor who was resident rather than just an overnight guest. More than ever, special functions became an important part of the hotel's business, requiring space and facilities to match the demands of the age.

Successive alterations were made over the years to modernise the bedroom accommodation and the public rooms. Such work often results in a loss of character, but fortunately the Georgian architectural style of the hotel that is in harmony with so much of Beverley was not swept away. Today's façade is eighteenth-century in style, but the spirit and tradition of the Beverley Arms strongly recalls its predecessor, the Blue Bell.

The exterior of the Beverley Arms.

BILTON: *GARDENERS ARMS*

Bilton: Leave Harrogate on A61 Ripon road. At Skipton roundabout turn right A59. In one mile turn left on Bilton Lane.

Suddenly modern houses and bungalows on the north-eastern fringe of Harrogate give way to real countryside; neat front gardens are replaced by open fields and grassy valleys. Without warning the sign for the Gardeners Arms appears round a bend of Bilton Lane and a handsome sign it is, showing the gardener at work, flanked by maidens carrying the fruits of his labour. Below are the words 'In the sweat of thy brows shalt thou eate thy bread'.

Below and behind the sign stands a little stone-built pub dating, it is thought, from 1698, with mullioned windows in the traditional style. Everything here testifies that small is beautiful, although the lawned

Exterior of the Gardeners Arms.

gardens to side and rear are exceptionally large and obviously popular, with many tables and seats. A background of trees and a narrow beck add to its attraction.

But it is the unaltered domestic feeling the pub has which must be its secret. The central passage has on its right the Parlour with a serving hatch; here may have been the landlord's family room. Across the passage is the largest of the 'business' rooms called the Piggery, where the regulars can sit round the huge and ancient fireplace. One of fifty years' standing recalled that it was once hidden behind a fireplace of little importance; fortunately it was opened up to show its glory. He was able to remember the days when the beck used to overflow and flood the pub.

All the rooms have comic names, but whether it is true that the name plates were designed for coffins may only be another slice of humour. Behind the Parlour is the tiny bar with an even tinier snug – a cupboard with a seat would be a fair description – and behind the Piggery is Wrinkley Lodge. The only explanation for this seems to be a picture on the wall of a curled-up sleeping dog carrying the legend 'Days like this give me Wrinkles'.

Again on a tiny scale is the Conservatory Club founded, as the plate alleges, on '8.8.88'. It is the Piggery and the flagged floors that give the best evidence of the age of the building, which looks today as it must always have done.

As a means of coping with drink orders from garden customers, a covered bar with a counter flap faces the lawn and beck; stone outbuildings line the two sides of the courtyard. Here is another fragment of history, as the major building houses the Franklin brewery which must once have been the pub's brewery. It is still operating as an independent concern.

The Piggery.

The passageway showing the flagged floor.

If all of this speaks of village identity and independence, Bilton people like it that way – rather than an address suggesting that it is a suburb of Harrogate. As a notice in the pub proclaims, Bilton was a separate village centuries before Harrogate's spring waters brought the town's growth; once, indeed, Harrogate's gas supply was dependent on coal mined at Bilton. There is some evidence that a small flax mill stood across the road from the Gardeners Arms using the waters of Bilton Beck for power; there were also bleach fields associated with the flax industry close by.

Two bachelor brothers, Richard and Francis Taylor, lived in an area now known as Bachelor Gardens. One of the brothers died and as a memorial the surviving brother founded a school for local children, which opened in 1793. The endowment was in the form of the brothers' orchards and gardens that provided the income for the school and it is probable that this is how the Gardeners Arms was named.

In the nineteenth century Bilton had a population of only a few hundred, mainly working in textiles, stone, or on the land. Today's regulars can still enjoy a pub that was very much a dwelling house, with the living rooms being used by its visitors.

BIRSTALL: *BLACK BULL INN*

Birstall: M62 J27, A62 south. At A652 turn right. In ½ mile church and Black Bull on left.

The Black Bull Inn, Birstall.

Position counts for so much where a pub is concerned and Kirkgate, Birstall, was in its heyday a road of great importance for the Black Bull as the route of the Leeds–Elland turnpike from its completion in 1740. Earlier still was a route, described in 1655 as 'The Stoney Causeway', also passing towards Leeds this way, so the Black Bull had an important location even before 1740. Today the Bradford–Dewsbury traffic streams past the end of Church Lane, leaving Kirkgate, the Black Bull and the parish church as an island surrounded by modern roads and buildings.

Facing St Peter's Church as it does, the Black Bull could serve churchgoers by catering for special events as well as the needs of travellers. As was usual with old pubs, the Black Bull was used for a variety of public functions: auctions, polling at elections, parish affairs and as a magistrates' court which sat upstairs in what is now the Function Room. The last case is believed to have been heard in 1839. When its purpose as a court was over, the furniture and panelling in the courtroom was allowed to remain, so the magistrates' chair and prisoners' box are well-preserved survivors. They have their original painted front panels and handsome canopies, creating a unique atmosphere for organisations such as Rotary which use the room for meetings today.

Most of the cases heard in the court at the Black Bull dealt with debt recovery, in spite of unlikely reports of prosecutions for crimes against the person leading to execution. Some of the wildest assertions involved local Luddites, said to have been accused of destroying new labour-saving machinery in textile mills. No court records support these allegations, or the belief that there were executions at Birstall for Luddite activity.

Perhaps more likely is a belief that the Brontë family went to the Black Bull when they were visiting Oakwell Hall, which is very close. Charlotte knew Birstall well

Oakwell Hall, Birstall.

through her friend Ellen Nussey whose home was here. Oakwell was introduced as Fieldhead in *Shirley* and Red House at Gomersal on the hill behind the Black Bull was Briarmains in *Jane Eyre*. Ellen Nussey is buried in St Peter's churchyard at Birstall, opposite the Black Bull.

On the end wall of the Black Bull is a stone with a curious inscription and carrying the date 1754. The wording leaves a good deal to the imagination; possibly it is a reference to some alterations made in 1754, while another theory is that it was a flood marker. In either case it may well have been moved from another position.

Although the Black Bull's history is some 400 years long, the town of Birstall goes back much further. Its name probably has an origin in the Saxon 'burh': a fortified settlement. 'Stall' has been variously defined as a homestead, or just a place.

BISHOP BURTON: *THE ALTISIDORA*

Bishop Burton: A1079 east from York via Market Weighton.

Pub names vary endlessly and may be changed for the oddest reasons, so that a pub with a long history sometimes has a name and a sign chosen in quite recent times. It was like this at Bishop Burton, where Altisidora faces the pool in this lovely village deep in the countryside.

There can hardly be a greater contrast with Yorkshire Dales scenery than the A1079 east of Market Weighton. Instead of dominant bare fells and narrow roads

THE ALTISIDORA

with passing places, here across Cherry Burton Wold there are fields of cereals and rolling open views to the far horizon. Although both distant landscapes appear lonely, the road from York to Beverley is always busy with traffic.

About 10 miles from Market Weighton the road curves gently down towards the centre of Bishop Burton, with Altisidora on the left surrounded by whitewashed cottages and beautifully kept gardens. On the village green an open air service is held each July to commemorate the occasion in the eighteenth century when John Wesley preached to a local gathering.

The pub is over 400 years old and is, according to Pevsner, 'consciously picturesque'. In fact, the whole village is exquisite. Close to Beverley, with the racecourse

The Altisidora . . .

. . . and its beautiful setting.

nearby, the Altisidora's clientele expects facilities of a high standard. In spite of the pub's age, the interior today is comfortably contemporary.

Originally the village was called South Burton, but became Bishop Burton because early archbishops of York had a palace in the parish. The manor of Bishop Burton was surrendered to the Crown at the Dissolution of the Monasteries and the estate then passed by sale and inheritance through several wealthy families. It was Richard Watt, the then lord of the manor, who renamed the pub Altisidora. That was the name of his racehorse, which won the 1813 St Leger and is pictured on the sign. By the 1950s the Hall and the estate at Bishop Burton were up for sale. After demolition a College of Agriculture was founded there with new buildings that opened their doors in 1954.

When you are at Bishop Burton, do not fail to visit All Saints' Church, high up behind the pool. Although some Norman parts remain, there has been a great deal of rebuilding, especially in the nineteenth century, when the famous architect of Truro Cathedral, J.L. Pearson, designed a new chancel. Look for the bust of John Wesley, carved from a tree that once stood on the green.

Allow time to go to South Dalton, taking a turn to Cherry Burton just on the Beverley side of the Altisidora. There it is possible to see more of the best work of J.L. Pearson, who was commissioned to build a new church by the third Baron Hotham in 1858. The 200ft slender spire can be seen from miles around reaching needle-like for the sky. The interior is in Pearson's High Gothic style. Such is the quality of the whole of this church that to choose one part of it as its very best is to invite disagreement. For many the sanctuary and east window are unsurpassed.

BOROUGHBRIDGE: *THE BLACK BULL*

Boroughbridge: A1M to J48, then follow the signs.

Once England's road system had begun to make wheeled traffic possible, Yorkshire ceased to be a generally isolated and thinly populated region. London was no longer only a destination for drovers who, with their cattle, were prepared to face the distance and unpaved, uneven tracks. Travel was still uncomfortable, but Yorkshire was becoming a realistic destination, as well as providing some of the many stops for road traffic going further north to Scotland.

Boroughbridge's position on what became the Great North Road certainly made it an important stop, but it was a thriving market town in its own right with a river crossing, always an important asset. Goods traffic using the river Ure from a wide rural area round about encouraged market activity; traders would have needed pubs like the Black Bull for food and accommodation, particularly at the time of cattle fairs.

The Black Bull had a vital part to play in the commercial life of Boroughbridge, as the pub yard and its stables extended a considerable distance down St Helena towards the river Tutt. Loading and unloading goods in the yard and handling the

The Black Bull, Boroughbridge.

horses was a large-scale activity, so the character of the Black Bull was that of a business establishment. It also provided facilities for coach passengers on the Thirsk to Harrogate run. The pub's front on cobbled St James' Square with its fountain shows the building to be of considerable age, probably dating back to the thirteenth century: a suggested date has been 1262.

The centrally placed door leads directly to an L-shaped bar. On the right an opened-up front room with a massive fireplace is now the lounge. Low medieval beams and low doors, especially to the snug, are a feature of the interior, as are the sloping bedroom floors. Getting in or out of bed is often an uphill journey! The restaurant is surprisingly large and has been beautifully furnished.

Ghostly happenings in pubs are by no means unusual and it is tempting to explain them through stories of past events that have been told and retold, losing nothing in the telling. The Black Bull is different – no history of quarrels, of death or of disappearance. Yet there is regular evidence even today of strange activity at the back of the pub, where the restaurant and several bedrooms now occupy the area where the stables once stood.

The landlord has a late night routine of setting the tables for residents' breakfasts; this includes turning the morning drink glasses upside down. Imagine his surprise one morning recently to find them turned over again; he was very careful the following evening to be sure that he had turned the glasses over as usual, only for them to be reversed by the morning. On another occasion he found table napkins

The fireplace at the Black Bull.

The fountain on
St James' Square.

spread out on the steps. The chef had his crockery moved off the kitchen table top, and once found his dishes spread out in a long line on the floor.

Late nights seem to be attractive for the naughty ghost, who moved chairs from under dining tables where they had been placed, just to be sure that the landlord would fall over them when he returned from taking his dogs out for a walk before bedtime – and not just on one occasion.

Only once has anyone or anything been seen; a resident woke to find a person wearing a cloak in his room, walking through a wall. It was real enough for him to phone the police!

Looking across St James' Square to the Black Bull it is easy to picture its past with coaches coming and going and passengers thronging the pub. Today modern comforts within blend well with ancient timbers. Change there has been: the coming of the railways affected the Black Bull's passenger and freight business, but the vast increase of road traffic since the Second World War and the development of tourism have restored prosperity. The Black Bull is as popular and busy as it has ever been.

BRADFIELD DALE: *STRINES INN*

Bradfield Dale: From M1 J35a, A616; after Underbank Reservoir turn left at Midhopestones, then follow signs.
OR From Sheffield A57 Manchester road, after Moscar Lodge turn right for Strines.

One of the great advantages Yorkshire folk enjoy explaining to the less fortunate from elsewhere is how quickly they can reach wonderful countryside from the largest towns and cities in the county. Life is too short for a list of even *some* of these, but Bradfield is a perfect example: only 7 miles from Sheffield in map mileage, but a world away in every other respect.

Bradfield comprises High Bradfield, Low Bradfield and Bradfield Dale, which could confuse the unwary motorist, particularly when bare moors, winding lanes and forested hills open up views of the reservoirs in the valleys. Maps need to be studied before setting out for Bradfield Dale to avoid going round in circles and seeing the same dam over and over again. With good reason the area has earned the title Sheffield's Lake District.

Strines Inn enjoys fabulous views, particularly down to Strines reservoir and from the hill above the pub eastwards to Bradfield Moors. Just west of the pub is a small watercourse called Strines Dyke flowing down to the reservoir; the pub's name must have come from this. Strines is an old English word meaning 'the meeting of water'.

Strines Inn at Bradfield Dale.

The fireplace at Strines Inn.

As far back as 1275 there was a building at 'Strynds', but its history as a manor house owned by the Worrall family really began in Elizabethan times. The oldest part of the present Strines is the central portion that would have consisted of the great hall, kitchen, buttery (for drinks), dairy and parlour. The massive fireplace would have been a prominent feature. At either end of the central block extensions were made later, resulting in a building of substantial size.

The Worralls were yeoman farmers and woollen clothiers (there is a Worrall village a few miles east of High Bradfield). Their coat of arms is above the entrance to Strines, but is almost hidden at present by climbing plants.

The long period of residence of the Worralls ended in 1771 when the building was leased to John Morton and became an inn. The road past Strines from Bamford to Penistone was wild and hazardous until 1775 when it was turnpiked and the ancient packhorse bridges were replaced.

It was while John Morton was landlord that the incident of the disappearing tailor took place. He stayed overnight and was known to have a large amount of gold with him. Both tailor and gold disappeared and were never seen again. Normally the nearest the pub came to a breach of the law was in allowing poachers to meet there.

By the late 1830s the Worrall family ended their connection with the pub by selling it to a Sheffield merchant, who in turn sold it to the Fitzwilliam family. Past landlords had farmed surrounding land, but in the 1961–81 period an agreement was reached granting landlords a lease on the pub in return for giving up the right to farm. This arrangement still stands today.

Twenty-first-century overnight guests at the Strines have all the comforts of en-suite accommodation, while the three areas for pub use of which the bar is the centre one are traditionally furnished and decorated. The Strines faces south towards the A57 road 3 miles away, its gable end on to the passing moorland road. A favourite table for meals looks out uphill towards the A57; on a warm day tables under the trees are a joy.

A last glimpse of the Strines from the hill above is a picture of continuity and country tradition. The Worralls were here for hundreds of years, and their manor house (now the Strines) was built of local material according to local ways; it is as much part of the landscape as the trees, grass and stone walls around it.

BURNSALL: *RED LION*

Burnsall: From Skipton A59 east to Bolton Bridge then B6160.

The stretch of the river Wharfe from Bolton Bridge upstream to Burnsall has the reputation – mightily well deserved – of being the most beautiful few miles in Yorkshire. As if to underline this, the view from above Burnsall is breathtaking. Down in a curve of the river overlooked by high Burnsall Fell, is the Red Lion, only a step or two from the handsome five-arched bridge. If ever there was a perfect location, this is it.

The Red Lion, Burnsall.

Front or back, the pub's windows look out on to a Wharfedale world of trees, grass and, above all, water, smooth and wide-flowing below the bridge, yet increasingly restless above it. The back terrace faces the river walk that goes upstream towards the 'rapids', miniature falls in the river's surface.

The sixteenth-century name for the Red Lion was the Ferryman's Inn, no doubt on account of a ferry there before the building of the bridge. Since the cellars date from the twelfth century, a pub certainly stood on the site even earlier – early enough for a well-established ghost whose activities include turning off the beer taps.

Today's Red Lion has plenty of beams and creaky sloping floors, a building much extended around the sixteenth-century area that includes the present bar. At the front door a notice asks countryside explorers to leave their walking boots outside. Well understood by the regulars who enjoy the many local walks, this precaution helps to protect the comfortably furnished and warmly decorated lounge as well as the fine restaurant.

This is the Craven district of Wharfedale which took its name from the Earls of Craven. The family title came from a local boy who made good called Dick Whittington. Born at nearby Appletreewick (which you *must* visit) of a poor family, he went to London, became apprenticed to a mercer, worked hard and eventually in 1610 became Mayor of London. He was knighted as Sir William Craven and his son was created Earl of Craven. Sir William 'butified' St Wilfrid's Church in Burnsall and erected the bridge, since rebuilt several times.

CAWOOD: *THE FERRY INN*

Cawood: A1M J45, then A64/A659 to Tadcaster town centre. Take A162 south towards Sherburn in Elmet. In about 3 miles turn left for Cawood B1223.

River crossings, whether by ford, bridge or ferry, encourage village settlements, attract road traffic and, naturally, pubs. Here at Cawood, some 5 miles from Selby, a road connection between east and west Yorkshire depended on some means of crossing the river Ouse. The river is tidal at Cawood – and deep at high tide – so a ferry would have been the original and only means of crossing.

The present sixteenth-century Ferry Inn adopted its name when the pub on the opposite bank of the river (where the ferry was based) closed its doors; it stands next to the swing bridge that takes today's traffic across the river. A stone-flagged floor, beamed ceiling and small rooms overlooking King Street to the front and the riverside garden at the back are those features of the pub that reflect its history.

Few pubs can show the history of the village as plainly as the Ferry Inn; on the wall is a plaque listing the events that took place, particularly at the Castle. Do not look for a powerful keep, battlements or a moat here, as Cawood Castle was 'slighted' on Cromwell's orders after the Civil War. What remains is a handsome, beautifully

Left: The Ferry Inn.
Below: The plaque in the Ferry Inn telling of Humpty Dumpty's great fall.

decorated gatehouse, flanked by farm buildings; much of the stone from the demolished castle was taken to York to extend the Archbishop's Palace at Bishopthorpe. Cawood's connection with York deserves special mention.

It was 1530 when Cardinal Wolsey came to Cawood Castle, en route to his planned and much delayed enthronement as Archbishop of York. He had made the big mistake of displeasing his king, Henry VIII, by failing to obtain an annulment of the royal marriage to Catherine of Aragon. What happened next is noted on the plaque in the Ferry Inn as 'Humpty Dumpty's great fall'.

While at Cawood, preparing to travel on to York, Wolsey was arrested for high treason on behalf of the king by the Earl of Northumberland. There is no doubt that he would have been executed had he reached London, but he died of dysentery at Leicester Abbey, his disgrace and downfall complete.

A curious aspect of this is a record that Mother Shipton of Knaresborough prophesied that Wolsey would see York, but would never get to the city. Seen as a confirmation of this prediction is a tradition that Wolsey looked out from the castle tower at Cawood and could see York in the distance. In the Great Hall of the Bishop's Palace at Bishopthorpe is a portrait of Wolsey: the archbishop who never was. Although Wolsey never reached York, at least stone from the ruined castle did, in order to extend the palace. Was this the long arm of coincidence?

There is a Wolsey walk at Cawood that begins near the bridge and the Ferry Inn, and includes the Castle Gatehouse and Wharfe's Mouth, where the rivers Wharfe and Ouse join. As a historic trail that can include the Ferry Inn, it may be highly recommended.

COXWOLD: *FAUCONBERG ARMS*

Coxwold: A19 York–Thirsk, turn right in 15 miles via Husthwaite.

Life is quiet and unhurried at Coxwold; time seems to pass more slowly there than anywhere else. The village's one street with its wide green borders and handsome stone cottages slopes gradually up from the crossroads to reach the parish church of St Michael on the brow of the hill.

Just below the church the pub stands out from even the larger houses because of its length, its deep forecourt paved with huge cobbles and the colourful arms of the Fauconbergs from whom its name comes. Until 1823 it had been the Bellasis Arms (sometimes spelt Bellasyse) from the family who owned Newburgh Abbey. Dr Anthony Bellasis was granted the estate at the Dissolution of the Monasteries and

The Fauconberg Arms at Coxwold.

left it to his nephew Sir William Bellasis, whose descendant Sir Thomas Bellasis was created Earl Fauconberg in 1682. The last Earl Fauconberg died in 1832 and the estate went to the Wombwell family by marriage.

It is firmly believed by many that Mary, daughter of Oliver Cromwell and wife of Viscount Fauconberg, had her father's remains brought to Newburgh after the Restoration in 1660 and buried in a secret tomb in one of the rooms.

Although the present Fauconberg Arms dates from the seventeenth century, an earlier business on the site would have been a village ale house for local traffic rather than a posting inn. The pub's gable, its porch with pillars and its many windows give a welcoming atmosphere, its identity proclaimed by the Fauconberg sign. Beautifully painted and fixed to the front wall, it shows the coat of arms, the family crest and their motto 'Bonne et Belle Assez'. Inside, the huge beams and fireplaces are truly authentic and the size of the flagstones in the floor has to be seen to be believed.

Faced with a bewildering choice of visits in and around Coxwold, a list of 'musts' should include Shandy Hall, the home of the former vicar and author Laurence Sterne, just above the pub.

On the opposite side of the road is the church with its unusual and attractive octagonal tower. It has many family monuments and effigies of the Bellasis family and should not be missed as they tell of their importance to the village and its history.

Beyond the village itself are Byland Abbey, the White Horse of Kilburn and the village workshop of 'Mousey' Thompson, the craftsman. Close by, of course, is Newburgh Abbey, once the Fauconberg home and open to the public.

CROPTON: *THE NEW INN*

Cropton: A1M to J49, then A168 to Thirsk, A170 via Helmsley to Wrelton.
At Wrelton turn north to Cropton.

Spreading in a great arc to the north of Cropton are the moors and forests of the North York Moors National Park. Separated from Appleby le Moors by the little river Seven, both villages are on the very boundary of the National Park, with Pickering a few miles to the south in much gentler countryside.

Pubs carrying the name 'New' are often thought to have had a name change at some time in the past. Not so here: the pub is said to date from the mid-eighteenth century and to have originated from a dwelling house that was converted to pub use. Unusually, the bar with beamed ceiling is upstairs, also the coffee lounge. The Lee family who have been here since 1986 offer nine en-suite bedrooms for residents and there is a well-appointed restaurant. The ground floor rooms are used for beer and food storage.

Beer has been brewed in the village since 1613. In 1984 a previous landlord, David Mullins, began brewing beer in the New Inn's basement. A story has grown that this was a response to local fears that in the worst winter weather beer supplies from distant breweries might not get through, but this seems to be unfounded. Whatever the facts, Cropton beer was such a wonderful brew that supplies were

The New Inn, Cropton.

Cropton beer pumps.

readily sold to other outlets. In 1994 Cropton Brewery opened at Woolcroft, the farmland behind the pub. Traditional and well-established methods are used and over ten different beers are currently brewed.

Of these beers the legendary Cropton Two Pints was an award winner in the Great British Beer Festival in 1995. It was the very first Cropton brew and still their most popular cask beer.

Another award winner is Scoresby Stout, named after William Scoresby who was born at Cropton in 1760. He became famous through his whaling voyages from Whitby to far northern oceans, recruiting Cropton men for his crew. In command of *Resolution* in 1806 he sailed north to just 510 miles from the Pole.

Scoresby would have known the New Inn and would have passed the pub on his way to and from Cropton. If only we could discover whether he visited, and signed on members of his crew in the bar!

Cropton Brewery.

DENBY DALE: *THE DUNKIRK*

Dunkirk: M1 J37 to Barnsley then A635 Huddersfield/Manchester.

There must be many pubs in England located at crossroads, often the only shelter available for miles around. It is tempting to picture the Dunkirk in earlier times as one of these solitary inns with a gallows for company that would have served as a reminder to wayfarers of the fate awaiting convicted felons.

On the contrary: today's pub was yesterday's dwellings in the tiny hamlet of Dunkirk in this outlying part of Denby Dale known as Lower Denby. The building was originally three traditional stone cottages of 1840 that faced the Waggon & Horses coaching inn across the road. Within fifty years the three cottages had been bought by the Cubley brewery of Thurlstone. One of the cottages had been a pub; the opening up of the interiors of all three allowed a conversion into more spacious premises.

By 1912 the Gill family had taken over the pub, naming it appropriately The Junction, as it stood on the Huddersfield to Barnsley road where the road to Penistone and Dry Hill Lane crossed the main highway. So small is Dunkirk that it must have seemed of little importance so far as the main focus of life, Denby Dale, was concerned. Separated on its hill from the main village down by the river Dearne and dependent on the bridge for contact, Denby Dale must have felt like another world to Dunkirk villagers.

Dunkirk Inn, Denby Dale.

Pie Hall.

In his book *Denby & District* Chris Heath speaks of the grass triangle opposite the Dunkirk and the stone building that used to stand there. This was known as the Salt Pile because it was used for the storage of salt brought to Dunkirk by packhorse and then distributed in the neighbourhood. Chris Heath's book suggests that the hamlet's name of Dunkirk originated as far back as 1658 when English troops were involved in war between France and Spain.

The giant pies baked since 1788 have brought Denby Dale international fame. Some idea of their amazing size can be seen from the monster pie dish outside the Pie Hall on the Wakefield road; this dish is now used as a flower bed! The recovery of King George III from his mental affliction provided a reason for baking the first pie; since then there have been nine more, each celebrating events of national importance such as Queen Victoria's Golden Jubilee in 1887. (This particular pie proved unfit to eat!) The most recent was the Millennium Pie in 2000. The 1964 pie and its celebration raised funds that led to the opening of the Pie Hall in 1972.

Only 4 miles or so away is Cannon Hall and its country park which attract many visitors, but there is history to be seen much nearer through the Dunkirk Inn's front windows. Just across the fields extensive stone buildings mark the position of Papist Hall, so called because of the Catholicism of the Blackburn family who once lived there. The barn which stands gable-ended to the approach lane was built in 1633. Behind the barn is a courtyard, and date stones in the wall provide confirmation as follows: 'Robart Blacke Burne 1633'. Below is the addition: 'Rebuilt by William Smith 1845'. Facing across the courtyard is the present owner's house, also of the

The pie dish that masquerades as a flower bed.

Papist Hall.

nineteenth century. Without doubt the Blackburns were a leading and influential family who played an active part in local history.

Dunkirk has had the benefit of its high location to be able to oversee the main activities along the river valley as well as in the surrounding countryside. On the skyline are two building masterpieces: the twenty-one arch railway viaduct completed in 1879 and the graceful TV mast on the far ridge at Emley. At a height of 1,080 feet it is the tallest concrete structure in Europe – a fitting match for Denby Dale's huge pies.

EAST MARTON: *THE CROSS KEYS*

East Marton: A65 Leeds to Skipton. At Skipton take A59 west. Keep on A59 at A59/A56 roundabout beyond Broughton.

True lovers of the countryside would not be able to resist the Cross Keys. Without its pub signs it might appear a farmhouse, which indeed it was in the seventeenth century, modest in size and totally in harmony with its land and the tiny community sharing the green where it stands. Like so many small country pubs in Yorkshire that served mainly local residents the pub business had to be combined with farming to make a living.

The L-shaped lounge and bar are spacious with internal walls gone, and the farmhouse atmosphere has been retained; beyond the bar to the front of the pub is a

The Cross Keys, East Marton.

The remarkable double-arch bridge over the Leeds–Liverpool Canal.

further area for meals and a comfortable drawing room. A recent extension to the rear with a view down to the canal is a non-smoking restaurant. Outside are tables and chairs for summer weather use.

It would be easy, but misleading, to explain the attraction of the Cross Keys by pointing to its country pub character and its position well back from the busy A59 Harrogate–Preston road and close to the A56 road to Burnley.

Far less obvious to the motorist, but familiar to the walker, is the Pennine Way which crosses the A59 at East Marton. Hardly noticeable too when driving is the double-arch bridge just down the hill that carries the A59 over the Leeds–Liverpool Canal; it is surprising to find the number of guests at the Cross Keys who have come with the one intention of walking to look at it. This is not by any means an ordinary double-arch bridge, as the arches are built one above the other, not end to end; it is said to be one of just three examples in the country. The story is that when the A59 road was constructed the bridge carrying the original turnpike was found to be inadequate for today's heavy traffic. Instead of altering the line of the road and putting in a new bridge close to the present crossing, a second arch was built above the early one.

A short walk down the lane by the side of the Cross Keys leads to the canal, one of the most attractive stretches of its 127-mile route. It winds its way through gaps in the hills past grazing land in the Aire Valley from Skipton and is very popular with narrow boat enthusiasts who can tie up at moorings just below the Cross Keys. From the moorings the double bridge is only 100 yards along the towpath with the Cross Keys on the hill close by.

The sloping fields on either side of the canal are homes for grazing horses; the farm by the footbridge near the moorings has a riding business. The farmhouse and the cottage beside it are clearly old, even older than the Cross Keys. The pub had a barn on its east side when it was a working farm, now converted into two houses with attractive gardens. Facing the green to the west of the pub are three seventeenth-century cottages, one of which was formerly a shop and the East Marton post office, which closed in the 1960s.

Cross Keys pubs are numerous in Yorkshire; other examples are in Goodramgate, York, and at Stillingfleet between Selby and York. Since York Minster and Ripon Cathedral are both dedicated to St Peter it would not be surprising to find his emblem, based on 'I will give you the keys of Heaven', on pub signs. The heraldic description is 'Two keys crossed in saltire': they are usually found with the wards of the keys facing upwards and outwards. St Peter is often included, as at East Marton, holding the keys. After the Reformation and the break with Rome some of the signs were changed and royal emblems, such as the Crown or the King's Head, were adopted in their place.

FOSTER BECK, PATELEY BRIDGE:
THE BRIDGE INN AND FORMER WATERMILL

Pateley Bridge: either from Harrogate A61 north to Ripley roundabout, then B6165; or from Skipton B6265 via Grassington.

Descriptions are useful, but risk becoming obvious. To call Pateley Bridge the gateway to Nidderdale is an example, as it is so much more. From Harrogate, Ripley and Summerbridge the car driver can look forward to a wonderfully scenic drive followed by a steep descent of the main street to the bridge over the Nidd; from Skipton, Grassington and Greenhow the route is wild and open while the drop to Pateley Bridge is even more hair-raising. One can imagine two drivers coming from opposite directions and breathing a sigh of relief as they meet eyeball to eyeball at the bridge. In both cases there is only one further route available: up Nidderdale towards the Bridge Inn.

In just over a mile the road swings left to the Bridge Inn standing beside a tiny bridge over Foster Beck that flows down to join the Nidd. Immediately on turning into the car park there is the sight of an extraordinary water wheel over 35ft in diameter at the end of a long stone building opposite. This huge wheel is said to be the largest in the north. The building was once a flax mill founded in 1720 to take advantage of the crops of flax for which the countryside was especially suitable. Until recently it was the Watermill pub, but no longer.

The Bridge Inn, Pateley Bridge.

The converted watermill.

Drastic change has taken place here. The mill has been converted into apartments, the water wheel having been restored. It does not turn any more but, motionless in the sunshine, the structure is a favourite place for the neighbourhood cats to bask. Log cabins have been added on the hill to increase the accommodation.

The pub has been transferred to the smaller mill house at the original entrance to the mill grounds by the bridge; this is not residential, but has a full range of meals and is comfortably furnished. The bar opens into an additional seating area where lunches are served, while beyond is a spacious restaurant where visitors and residents in the converted accommodation may dine.

The old days of the watermill are recalled with a number of photographs on the walls of the Bridge Inn. One shows a mill worker processing flax and an aerial photograph gives a good impression of the estate when the mill was in operation. For lovers of massive shire horses there is a large colour reproduction of a brewery dray making a delivery here. Turning the bend in the road bordered by stone walls and approaching the pub on a misty morning, these fine animals are a reminder of times past and gone.

Having eaten at the Bridge Inn, the visitor has the whole of Nidderdale to see – and there is a great deal – more than enough to bring a Dales lover back again and again.

HARDEN: *THE MALT SHOVEL*

Harden: A650 Bradford to Bingley. At church turn left B6429. In Harden take left turn towards Wilsden.

Although the pub name Malt Shovel can be found at a number of locations in Yorkshire, each has a different character and history. The Harden Malt Shovel was once part of the estates owned by Rievaulx Abbey; after the suppression of the monasteries ownership of the manor passed into lay hands. In 1676 the de Ferrand family bought Harden Grange and became the major landlord in the district, owning the Malt Shovel until the turn of the twentieth century.

The Ferrands' estate, now known as St Ives, was purchased on behalf of the public in 1918 and opened for a variety of uses: a golf club is based there and the grounds of St Ives provide for fine walks, public events and shows of all kinds.

The Malt Shovel at Harden.

The bridge by the Malt Shovel.

The Malt Shovel, too, has had a varied role. As probably the oldest pub in the area, its site has in its time been a farmhouse, coaching house, court room and a prison. Take a meal in the snug; it was once a cell for prisoners and has a massive fireplace that is believed to date back to the reign of William and Mary. It was discovered in the course of restoration work in the pub in 1980.

Unlike some pubs used as courtrooms, the Malt Shovel was visited by travelling 'hanging' judges who had the power to condemn those convicted of a serious crime to death by hanging. These sentences were carried out on Harden Moor and included penalties on highwaymen who lay in wait for their victims on the old Lancashire to Yorkshire road.

Another serious offence that carried the death penalty was that of 'whittling', which was clipping or shaving gold coins; the clippings were then melted down for turning into counterfeit coins. This seems to have been a criminal activity that was not uncommon in the area.

Not far away in the Calder Valley in the eighteenth century a notorious gang called the Cragg Coiners of Cragg Vale were doing much the same thing. Led by David Hartley, later executed at York, the gang of about seventy terrorised the neighbourhood, operating from remote farmhouses above Mytholmroyd. It is tempting to wonder if there was any criminal connection between the Whittlers of the Harden district and the Cragg Coiners of the Calder Valley.

It is more pleasant to remember the Malt Shovel for its other roles: as a farm it no doubt had its own brewhouse and malthouse, hence its name. It is of considerable age, has a warm traditional appearance and a lovely location by the bridge where the Wilsden road crosses Harden Beck. For exercise after good food, the visitor can do no better than to cross the bridge from the pub and follow the footpath by the beck to Goit Stock waterfall.

HAWORTH: *BLACK BULL*

Haworth: At the top of Main Street.

On a good day anyone having climbed up the famously steep Main Street to reach the Black Bull on the little cobbed square at its summit will have enjoyed some of the most magnificent views in West Yorkshire. Whether downhill towards Oxenhope or in brief glimpses of a distant world of moorland and stone walls through passages between houses, here is a real Brontë land. On another day, the setts paving the street shining with rain, Haworth is a different place, gloomy and melancholy. The atmosphere of the village on such a day seems closer to the Brontë legend than at any other time.

Like houses and cottages around it, the pub is built of gritstone darkened by smoke from the local mills during the nineteenth century. The mill chimneys have gone and clean air has returned, but Haworth remains an industrial village in countryside of

Right: The Black Bull at Haworth.
Below: The Brontë Parsonage Museum, former home of the gifted family.

Branwell Brontë's chair, kept at the Parsonage Museum. *(© The Brontë Society)*

great beauty. Fortunately the traditional character of the Black Bull has also been kept alive; in past days it was a centre for social life when there was no TV, radio or cinema.

Branwell Brontë came often to the Black Bull, welcomed by the landlord Thomas Sugden and his wife as an entertaining guest whose company was greatly enjoyed by everyone. No doubt Branwell found life at the Parsonage stifling and boring, so the Black Bull would have been a sanctuary for him.

It is said that if the vicar came to the pub asking if Branwell was on the premises, he would make a quick getaway via the back door or the kitchen window, thus allowing the landlord to give the vicar a truthful and innocent reply. In the Brontë Parsonage Museum is Branwell's favourite chair from the Black Bull.

The Black Bull stands near the church on the hilltop at Haworth. Another nice story linking pub and church tells how one past vicar, William Grimshaw, would set his choir and congregation singing a long hymn or psalm, then rush out to the Black Bull to whip drunkards there into church like a one-man press gang. Such is the history and rich is the character of Haworth and the Black Bull.

HEATH: *KING'S ARMS*

Heath: M1 J40 for Wakefield, on A638 continue towards Doncaster. After railway bridge fork left A655, left again for Heath.

Exterior of the King's Arms, Heath.

Until 1841 the village of Heath had no pub. The conversion of a row of cottages and stables in that year would not be enough for historians to reach for their pens, except that for many years the local pub had been the Cheesecake Inn a mile away at Kirkthorpe. One hot day in 1841 supplies of ale ran out, causing such a disturbance that the inn lost its licence, which was transferred to the cottages at Heath.

A delightful fragment of local history explains the name of the inn at Kirkthorpe, where hot, freshly baked cheesecakes were sold on Saturday mornings, hence Cheesecake Inn. The cottages at Heath which became the King's Arms are thought to have been built in about 1745, although a datestone over a neighbouring cottage door shows 1725, so the King's Arms may well be older than first thought.

Facing the extensive village green, the King's Arms is just where a pub ought to be. Its neighbours are not solely those of an agricultural community as five elegant houses overlook the green, including Heath House, designed by James Paine in 1744. The Old Hall, sadly, was demolished in 1961; built in 1595, it had become derelict. The number of major houses in such a small community is highly unusual, but must be the result of Heath's beautiful setting.

Just below the colourful pub sign is a gas lamp, signalling that the public rooms are all gas lit; suggestions to convert to electricity have been vigorously opposed by everyone. Open fires and a real Yorkshire range emphasise the pub's countryside character and the story of W.G. Grace playing an exhibition cricket match on the green completes a picture of complete rural bliss.

The bar of the King's Arms.

The fireplace at the King's Arms, showing the carved coat of arms.

The panelled restaurant of the King's Arms.

The King's Arms was tenanted successively by several families, the last of which was the Wrights, from 1924 to 1989. All of them seem to have been people of real character: Percy Wright's daughter, Dorothy, for example, who took over from her father in 1938 and was landlady for more than thirty years. She was a formidable lady who forbade under-age drinking and bad language.

Dorothy's brother Alan, only 5ft 3in tall and deaf and dumb, was nevertheless a very strong man; if anyone was heard using bad language, Alan would point a finger at him and raise it to his lips. It is said that no one ever dared to face the consequences of Alan's disapproval. Dorothy's nephew David Kerr became the licensee in 1969. He must have been an extraordinarily talented man, as he made furniture and the wall panelling in the pub, and carved the royal coat of arms as well as those of his family in the lounge. The two fireplace surrounds were originally upper sections of stone door frames he obtained from the now-demolished Heath Old Hall.

In the 1960s the King's Arms was extended; until then there were only two public rooms. The one on the left of the entrance door is about 12ft square. To the right, facing the old bar, is a tiny area known as the 'corfoyle', with seating for four people; only privileged locals were allowed there. In total contrast a new conservatory at the rear is very spacious, and the handsome panelled restaurant has accommodation extensive enough for functions.

All this and a ghost as well! Dame Mary Bolles, an ardent Royalist and philanthropist, who founded and funded the village School House in about 1637, lived at Heath Old Hall. On her death in 1662 she left instructions that her heart be buried in a casket in Kirkthorpe churchyard nearby; her other remains were to be entombed at Ledsham church, and the White Room where she died was to be walled up for ever. In spite of this it was reopened over fifty years later, and her spirit in the form of a grey lady is said to walk around the area of the Hall. Fortunately she does not seem to have visited the King's Arms – yet.

HELMSLEY: *THE BLACK SWAN*

Helmsley: On A170 from Thirsk to Scarborough.

Looking out on to the activities of the Market Place at Helmsley, the Black Swan's buildings stand on the site of an inn that was there centuries earlier. As an important road junction in Ryedale and a focal point for all local doings, Helmsley was once a centre for wool and for hand weaving in both wool and linen. The Black Swan would have been an unloading point for the fleeces brought from farms on the North York Moors.

But that was two hundred years ago. Life has moved on and the Black Swan with it, becoming an important coaching inn in 1838, serving the route from Leeds and York to Helmsley. The movement of people in increasing numbers pointed the way forward.

The charming exterior of the Black Swan Hotel.

To meet the developing needs of travellers – and later of tourists – visiting Helmsley Castle, Duncombe Park and Rievaulx Abbey as well as the wonderful Ryedale countryside, extensions to the Black Swan became essential. In 1947 the elegant Bankin's House was added and the Tudor black and white former rectory was incorporated seven years later. Now the Black Swan occupies the whole of the northern end of the Market Place, having the black and white house on the left, the Georgian house in the middle and the original Elizabethan building on the right: a rare and attractive combination.

Within, the Tudor house's oak beams and wattle and daub walling are exposed; the Georgian house reveals its fine stylish staircase. The Elizabethan part of today's building still has many traditional timbered ceilings, fireplaces and interior walls, while the Jacobean panelling came from the parish church during its nineteenth-century rebuilding. Of much more ancient origin is the Tudor stone entrance to the cellars, which came from Helmsley Castle ruins.

Truly the Black Swan has developed from an inn of great character to a modern hotel of fine style.

HUBBERHOLME: *THE GEORGE INN*

Hubberholme: From Skipton B6160, beyond Buckden fork left.

Upper Wharfedale is a world of its own. The narrow winding road from Buckden to Hubberholme would eventually take the traveller to Hawes, 10 miles further on. With glorious scenery all round and excellent walks from the George, this tiny peaceful hamlet attracts many visitors. At its very centre, the bridge over the Wharfe has the pub on one side and the church on the other; a farm near the bridge and a few scattered stone houses, and that is Hubberholme.

When the coaches to and from Lancaster once passed this way, passengers must have heeded the bridge, but little else as Hubberholme was left behind. The grey limestone church of St Michael and All Angels goes back to the twelfth century and has a painted rood loft of 1558, a rare treasure. The only other comparable example in Yorkshire is at Flamborough, and both probably escaped destruction because of the remoteness of their location. The pews are much later and are the work of Robert ('Mousey') Thompson of Kilburn, whose carved mice are much in evidence.

The George, like so many pubs, is close to the church, but has a very unusual link with it, as it was at one time used as a vicarage and a farm. Each January the Hubberholme 'Parliament' meets at the pub when an auction is held for the letting to farmers of 16 acres of grazing called the 'poor pasture', owned by the church. At the start of the bidding a candle on the bar is lit and remains so throughout the auction. The proceeds go to the elderly and poor of the parish.

Tradition is a word that should not be used lightly; here it is well justified, as the Hubberholme 'Parliament' has a history that stretches back over 1,000 years. The

Exterior of the George Inn.

Upper Wharfedale at Hubberholme.

name Hubberholme itself has its origins in Viking times when Hubba was a local leader who settled here.

The George's original flagged floors, beamed rooms and open fires must have appealed to J.B. Priestley who loved it. A memorial in the church says that his ashes are buried close by.

HUDDERSFIELD:
THE HEAD OF STEAM AND THE STATION TAVERN

M62 J23 then A640, or J24 then A629 to ring road, then follow signs to railway station.

There will be many people on their first visit to Huddersfield who, on entering George Square, will look at the railway station in disbelief and ask how the town could possibly have acquired a building of such quality and size and in such a setting. Sir John Betjeman described it as 'the most splendid station façade in England'.

There was early resistance to the development of railways in the nineteenth century by many investors in canal companies, and none more so in the Huddersfield area than by the powerful and influential Ramsdens, who had canal interests. Ultimately this view changed and one of the trustees of the Ramsden family estate, the Earl Fitzwilliam, commissioned his own architect, J.P. Pritchett of York, to design Huddersfield station.

Completed in 1850 to Pritchett's design in a Greek style, it has a huge central block with an imposing portico joined on both sides to pavilions through colonnades. The pavilions were intended to serve as booking offices for the Lancashire & Yorkshire Railway and the Huddersfield & Manchester Railway & Canal Company, both of which originally used Huddersfield station.

In the course of time there was a change in the use of the buildings: the central block became a general booking hall, allowing the Lancashire & Yorkshire Railway Company offices to become a refreshment room. Thus it remained until new ideas produced the pub facilities we have today.

The Head of Steam: After a big renovation project in the original L&Y offices, the Head of Steam opened its doors in 1996, having four rooms, each with its own character. With direct entrances from Platform 1 as well as from George Square, the pub acts as the main station buffet, with special arrangements for food and, of course, for opening hours. The buffet is a remarkable railway museum room; the family room has more railway artefacts; the lounge has a big collection of advertising enamels and is used for live music.

The imposing exterior of the Head of Steam.

Interior of the Head of Steam.

The bar houses antique advertising posters, a neon sign collection and art exhibitions. The Head of Steam has probably the best display of genuine railway artefacts in the north after the National Railway Museum at York. This includes nameplates, headboards and signalbox boards; there are even two live steam loco models.

Both railway enthusiasts and lovers of live music are well served; there is a live blues performance every Monday evening.

As a real ale pub the Head of Steam has a spot on the Penistone Line Pub Trail, which links Huddersfield with Barnsley and Sheffield. The Penistone Line Partnership is a voluntary organisation set up to encourage and promote community involvement in this route, which has magnificent viaducts and offers wonderful views. Together with the rail company, the PLP issues an information leaflet combining a map and details of the pubs near fifteen stations on the 37-mile Huddersfield to Sheffield line.

Station Tavern: Occupying the right-hand pavilion of the railway station façade, the Tavern was, like the Head of Steam at the opposite end, once a booking office – in this case for the Huddersfield & Manchester Railway and Canal Company. The company's handsome coat of arms remains above the front of the pavilion.

Until the 1960s it was a refreshment room, but its closure meant an alternative use of the rooms for parcels, storage and general station purposes. In 1979 the

The coats of arms of the rail companies originally using Huddersfield station.

Tavern was reopened in its present form, with one large seating area in front of the main bar with a 'snug-like' corner and side bar for drinks. A raised area on the railway platform side of the room is available for live entertainment.

Although its main business is for drinks, traditional pie and peas lunches are available at weekends and there is live music on Saturday nights. It is listed on the Penistone Line Pub Trail.

HULL: *YE OLDE WHITE HARTE*

Ye Olde White Harte, Silver Street: city centre via Whitefriargate, Park and Ride recommended; alight opposite Marks & Spencer.

If any contrast were needed with the timeless feel of pubs and villages in Yorkshire's wide acres of countryside, it can be found here at Kingston upon Hull, to give the city its full and correct title. As a great seaport Hull suffered grievously from bombing in the Second World War; afterwards the work of clearance, then postwar 'development' led to the disappearance of many buildings of character and historic interest.

This was especially true of the pubs; at one time Whitefriargate could boast six pubs, but it is now a shopping street similar to many in other large towns and cities. To see an example of what used to be, look above Boots the Chemist and a bargain book store to see the elegant façade of the 1794 Neptune Inn. Its large Venetian window, central decorated panel and arched windows tell of the richness of decoration within.

Ye Olde White Harte in Hull.

Once at the foot of Whitefriargate and on into Silver Street it will be necessary to look carefully for the White Harte sign at the end of a passage leading off to the pub entrance – and what a surprise! A small inviting courtyard with tables and chairs is surrounded by greenery and flowers that conceal the buildings that overlook this oasis.

The White Harte's architectural style both inside and out suggests a date in the seventeenth century; the Dutch-style gables and the fine oak staircase are strong evidence of this. One authority gives a building date of 1550, but if this were true many alterations would have had to be undertaken. The most likely origin of the White Harte is as a dwelling house built for Alderman William Foxley in the 1660s, becoming a pub in 1778.

The building date does have historic importance, since there is considerable folklore suggesting that the White Harte was the residence of the Governor of Hull during the Civil War. Tradition holds that the governor's house was involved with the refusal of the then governor, Sir John Hotham, to allow King Charles I entry to the city on 23 April 1642.

Recent study has concluded that the pub was the deputy governor's residence in 1688, when the Catholic Governor of Hull tried to arrest the governor's officers at the time when Prince William of Orange was expected to land in England. But whether the plot (if there was one) was hatched in the Plotting Parlour at the Olde White Harte has to remain the stuff of legend.

The fireplace of the Plotting Parlour.

The Plotting Parlour is on the first floor of the pub and is oak-panelled; outstanding is the elaborately carved overmantel wth two old swords in front of it that were discovered during alterations to the premises. Opposite on the first floor is the restaurant with pine panelling.

On the ground floor are the two bars: the main bar has a massive fireplace with the head of a stag above it and good stained glass, while the small saloon bar has behind it another of the pub's mysteries – a human skull in a perspex case. Once part of a skeleton found during renovations, the skull had a turbulent existence, even after death.

The entire skeleton was sent to the Hull Museum; however, bombing during the Second World War caused so much damage that the skull alone was recovered afterwards. It was returned to the White Harte, where it still causes much curiosity.

Of the several stories told to account for the skeleton, the most likely seems to be that a youth was the loser in a brawl with some sea captain whose violence in drink was enough to do mortal injury – accidentally perhaps? It is said that the body was sealed away, only for the hiding place to be discovered many years later.

HULL: *YE OLDE BLACK BOY*

Ye Olde Black Boy, 150 High Street: As for Ye Olde White Harte. Continue down Silver Street and Scale Lane to High Street.

An address on High Street would raise expectations of a pub surrounded by busy shops and shoppers. True, the market in Hull is close by, also Hepworth's Arcade of 1894 with elegant shops, but High Street has lost the importance it once had. Pevsner's reaction was 'What a High Street! Narrow, winding with desolation at the south end and a north end as if this was Wapping.'

High Street runs almost parallel to the waterfront on the river Hull so its buildings have been connected with trade; warehouses and legal and financial offices lined the street, with narrow staiths (or lanes) leading to the river. Close to the Black Boy is Maister's House of 1743, once the home and business premises of an important merchant family, now in the guardianship of the National Trust.

Like Maister's House, the Black Boy is a survivor, also of the eighteenth century. Its narrow frontage gives it the impression of being squeezed into its site, with greater and sometimes grander buildings all around. The Black Boy sign hanging over the pavement is that of an Indian chief, sometimes found as a standing model outside a tobacconist's shop. It is likely that a number of innkeepers started in business selling pipes and tobacco; in an 1888 letting of these premises a pipemaker's shop was included. The Indian chief sign of a tobacco merchant was probably familiar to passers-by here.

A 1904 plan of the pub sent to the licensing magistrates by Warwick & Co. was accompanied by a description of their business as 'Wine, Spirit & Cigar Merchants'

Ye Olde Black Boy in Hull.

The bar at Ye Olde Black Boy.

and as 'agents for champagne, Egyptian cigarettes and favourite blends of Scotch whiskey at the lowest prices'.

The site of the Black Boy seems to have had licensed premises in the 1720s and the pub name is first mentioned in 1748. Although over the next hundred years other merchants used the address, 150 High Street, in the Old Town, by the end of the nineteenth century the Black Boy was on a list of licensed premises as a free house and thus a familiar landmark on High Street.

By the twentieth century the Black Boy was a regular meeting place for businessmen, who could drink in the bar on the ground floor and have their formal meetings in one of the two meeting rooms on the upper floor.

Although a number of internal alterations were carried out in 1926 and there was a refurbishment in the 1990s, the general arrangements have remained: two rooms on both floors and a ground-floor passage to the rear. The similarity with the Blue Bell in York is striking.

Much of the ground floor panelling dates from 1926; upstairs there are two original fireplaces with interesting softwood surrounds and overmantels. These are in the eighteenth-century style, but they are more likely modern additions.

Such is the uncertain life for pubs today that it is encouraging to see the Black Boy flourishing; no doubt the support of organisations such as CAMRA in Hull will ensure its continued survival.

KELD: *TAN HILL INN*

Tan Hill: Reeth, Arkengarthdale via Langthwaite.

Standing on the summit of Stainmoor between Reeth and Brough, Tan Hill is 1,732ft above sea level. It is not only the highest inn in England, but must also be one of the remotest, with no village nearer than 5 miles.

Unique is a bold claim, but deserving in this case, as the pub overlooks mile after mile of empty moorland with distant spectacular views of the landscape of County Durham. In winter Tan Hill can be cut off by snowdrifts, sometimes for many days. In the severe winter of 1963 the family here was marooned for seven weeks. To cope with such a possibility it is needful to have a good food store, ample supplies of bottled gas and a generator for power. It goes without saying that a fire is always burning in the bar. Taking all the possible hazards into account, living here is not for the faint-hearted.

In such an exposed position the pub's 3ft thick stone walls and strong porch give some protection from the winter winds. Low-beamed ceilings and stone-flagged floors show how little change has taken place over the years.

An account of 1586 records a solitary inn on this site. When it was built there was an important crossroads here: cattle drovers, packhorse journeys, carriers with lead ingots from Swaledale mines and coal from Tan Hill's own colliery must all have

The solitary Tan Hill Inn.

A closer view of the exterior . . .

. . . and the welcoming interior of the Tan Hill Inn.

come this way. Amazingly, Tan Hill has survived to meet the needs of motorists and of walkers: the Pennine Way passes the door.

'Tan' is old Celtic for 'fire'. Possibly this high point was once used as a beacon position. If so, who used it, where was the next beacon and what messages were passed on here?

Wild and lonely as Tan Hill is in mid-winter, the Pennine Way walkers are on the move whenever that is possible – even when the weather shows signs of breaking. If that does happen, suddenly the bar can become full. Shelter is everything.

The big event of the year is in late May when the annual Sheep Show is held outside the pub. The business on that day is some compensation for all those winter days when there is not a single customer in sight, nor a great chance of business at the bar.

KIRKHEATON (OR 'YETTON'): *THE BEAUMONT ARMS*

Kirkheaton: From Huddersfield A642 Wakefield road. At A629 junction keep left, turning left immediately. In half mile at T junction turn right up hill. On right Church Lane (Beaumont Arms sign on corner).

The pub has had this name since 1803. Richard Beaumont of Whitley Beaumont Hall was lord of the manor at that date, although the Beaumonts were here for centuries. Memorials to early Beaumonts are in the parish church; of special interest is the effigy of 'Black Dick' or Sir Richard Beaumont who died in 1631. His colourful life has given rise to a number of legends, including one of haunting in the church's Beaumont Chapel. Another mysterious story has been attached to the decorated southern gateway to the church, known as Dead Man's Gate, bringing bad luck to those passing through it, especially couples marrying in the church. By the gate facing the pub is a monument to the tragic deaths of seventeen children, all girls, who died in a factory fire at Colne Bridge in 1818.

Locally the pub is known as Kirkstile, and is claimed to have been the ancient church house where festivals were held and parishioners took refreshment after Sunday services at the church before long journeys home across the extensive parish.

The memorial to the seventeen girls.

As far back as 1720 a survey recorded a building on this site with stables attached. While the stabling was useful for horses belonging to churchgoers, they attracted wrongdoers and dissolute people, becoming a common nuisance and a disgrace. The church-wardens were authorised to sell the stables. They themselves were not beyond criticism through their drinking at Kirkstile at the public expense; although attempts were made to stop it, they cannot have been successful, as 1826 brought an effort to limit the quantity of drink involved!

The manor court was held here, also the magistrates' court in early days. The building must have been used as a gaol too, as the stone base of a bed was found in the cellar. It was clearly a centre of village life. An interesting law enforcement organisation

Dead Man's Gate: its use was believed to bring bad luck.

was set up at the pub, called the Kirkstile Prosecution Society. Members paid for the employment of a private constable, fees being charged according to the value of an individual's property. This system continued until the middle of the nineteenth century.

Another quite different society called the Green Leaf met in the Squire's Room; this name came from the evergreen buttonholes the members wore when going out to sing carols at Christmas. Money they collected went towards providing an old folks' treat.

The present building of 1741 includes a window in the cellar that was part of an earlier seventeenth-century inn. Originally there were six low rooms downstairs and four chambers upstairs, also three cellars. No evidence has been found to support the belief about a secret passage connecting Kirkstile with the church across the road.

A large scale remodelling of the interior took place in 1930 and was carried out with some care. There was new attractive panelling, but the Squire's Room disappeared, as well as the great open fireplace with its chained poker. What does remain is a display of ancient documents including building accounts for the Beaumont Arms and the landlord's account for supplying hops and liquor to Whitley Hall. The Justices' expenses at the Kirkstile are listed, also the churchwardens' accounts at the Kirkstile including the supply of communion wine. One wonders if the churchwardens' drinking sessions were covered in this!

LEEDS: *WHITELOCKS*

Leeds, Turk's Head Yard, Briggate: First turning below the corner of Commercial Street and Kirkgate. The Yard leads through to Lands Lane.

For some, a visit to Raffles at Singapore would be the experience of a lifetime. Others, no doubt from Yorkshire, would value a meal at Whitelocks in Leeds far above anything exotic in the east. Who needs Raffles when we have Whitelocks?

Why should this be? How a family's enterprise and vision achieved so much is a story that needs to be told. In a world of rapid and radical change, the atmosphere the Whitelocks created and the standards they maintained survive today. The survival of an institution like Whitelocks will always be in danger from those who want change for change's sake and who have little respect for tradition because it is rooted in the past.

Whitelocks as a pub and the Whitelock family are part of Leeds history. Like a number of other pubs in the centre of the city, many of which are no more, it is located in one of the inn yards that became a feature of Leeds' development as it became an industrial centre. Briggate, or Bridge Street, leading northward from the crossing of the river, was originally laid out in a series of 'burgage plots', which eventually became inn yards with densely packed cottages alongside.

Even today it is possible to find the Ship Inn in Ship Inn Yard, the Pack Horse in Pack Horse Yard and the Turk's Head in Turk's Head Yard. It was the latter that in due course came to be known as Whitelocks. The reason for the early inn names is lost in the mists of time. As change followed change some of the inn yards disappeared through building developments, others went 'upmarket' and were converted into high-class shopping arcades, such as Thornton's Arcade in 1877 and Queen's Arcade in 1900.

As the Turk's Head, the pub had its first licence in 1715, though the building dates back further to the previous century. The story of the pub as Whitelocks begins, of course, with the first member of the family to hold the licence: John Lupton Whitelock. He was followed by William Henry Whitelock and Lupton Whitelock, who had an international reputation as a flautist.

Lupton was one of the first people to make a recording using a cylinder, and played for orchestras up and down the country, including the Hallé. At that time Whitelocks was frequented by many famous musicians and conductors, including

Whitelocks in Leeds.

Sir John Barbirolli and Sir Malcolm Sargent. Celebrities of the day from the Grand Theatre such as Dame Margot Fonteyn and Dame Anna Neagle visited the pub, as did journalists and artists. Sir John Betjeman much enjoyed Whitelocks, Jacob Kramer spent a good deal of time there and painted most of the family. Clearly, the pub was the centre of musical and artistic life in Leeds.

There is one sad story concerning Lupton Whitelock, who owned a splendid car with the registration UM 8425. He stood chatting with friends by the car one day and laid his silver flute on the running board, got in the car and drove off, never to see his flute again.

In 1886 Lupton altered the bar and dining room into what it is today. Little or no change has taken place in the last hundred years and this has been helped by a preservation order on both the inside and outside of the building. It has meant that the stained glass, mirrors, the marble-topped and tiled bar and the Art Nouveau brasswork dating back to Lupton's day are still there. The panelled dining room is through the curtains at the end of the bar. In Lupton's time Whitelocks had a doorman, an Irish giant, whose duties included turning away any gentleman not wearing a dinner jacket. Women were not allowed to stand at the bar, so waiters were employed.

Engraved on the pillar mirrors in the bar are prices of food: Sausages & Potatoes 3d, Cheese and Biscuits 1d, Pies 2d. A look at past and present menus shows that the

Whitelocks' dining room.

food is still essentially English, such as Whitelocks steak pie and jam roly poly with custard. The giant Yorkshire puddings and gravy are a joy to behold: not for nothing did – and does – Whitelocks deserves its early name still on the door: the First City Luncheon Bar (illustrated on page 9).

Cathy has been a waitress in the Dining Room for thirty years; her tables are as immaculate as her lacy apron, and her kindness has brought her innumerable friends. Such is her dedication that she has completed a list of landlords since 1770; and you will never be short of gravy if you have the privilege of dining at one of her tables. She has also become aware of a 'presence' in the cellars; there is no evidence of any event down there to explain the presence and fortunately he/she has never ventured upstairs.

Successive generations of the Whitelock family took over the licence until finally the pub was sold to Scottish & Newcastle Breweries in 1944, bringing to an end the Whitelocks' reign. The survival of the pub as Lupton intended is a tribute to the family. Their talents were considerable and one wonders what they would have achieved if their lives and careers had taken a different turn.

In the 1999 Good Pub Guide awards Whitelocks was listed as Town Pub of the Year, underlining the reputation it maintained for ninety years as a family business. It would be a mistake, however, to think that as a family the Whitelocks saw change happening around them, did not like what they saw and determined to resist it.

The pub was the first establishment in Leeds to have electricity and an electric clock. The clock in the dining room to the left of the fireplace is a good timekeeper. It has a secret too, as the space behind it became a favourite place for the pub cat to bring her kittens into the world. William Henry Whitelock, the second family licensee, installed a security device that would have delighted today's crime prevention authorities. Probably the health and safety inspectors would have been appalled, though. He installed an electric wire around the top of the bar where there was a fine display of roast beef, ham and Cornish pasties to dissuade customers from helping themselves to a free lunch. Modern thinking!

LEEDS: *THE VICTORIA HOTEL*

The Headrow to the Town Hall, then to rear: Great George Street.

By age and by location, the Victoria could not be more different from a typical Yorkshire country pub.

Built in 1865 to accommodate people attending the newly opened assize court at Leeds Town Hall immediately opposite, this is Victoriana in both age and style. Indeed, the Queen herself only a few years before opened the new Town Hall, designed to house the assize court.

These were times when the motor car was only a distant dream and the many people who came into Leeds on court business would have needed refreshment and overnight stay facilities. Such was the scale of business that the Victoria offered twenty-eight bedrooms as well as dining and recreation rooms, bars and private sitting rooms. On the upper floors were public meeting rooms.

Little more than thirty years later the Victoria Hotel Company went into liquidation and the building then changed hands twice. Why is a puzzle, as twentieth-century changes had not yet arrived, especially fierce competition as in today's hotel business. Perhaps it was poor management. The Vic's future became even more perilous when its demolition was proposed as part of development plans for Leeds city centre.

Fortunately, public protests from near and far, including from abroad, saved it and in the 1980s it was refurbished, retaining its splendid Victorian features. By a huge stroke of luck its original sign dating back to the 1890s was found covered by boards. It was sent for restoration, using gold leaf for the lettering and solid mahogany for its base.

The Victoria's imposing entrance with marble pillars catches the imagination and leads to bars on the left and right, each serving a different type of customer. Legend suggests that the legal profession always used the right-hand bar, while those with activities close to, or on the wrong side of the law, went to the left.

It is the 'lawyers' bar that is an elaborate feast of woodwork, providing private booths that can be reserved for colleagues to meet and eat.

The Victoria Hotel.

The Victorian interior of the Victoria.

At the back of seats in the booths are swivelling windows which when closed would allow for confidential legal discussions. When open one can only conclude that conversations going on are non-legal – golf stories perhaps?

If this all seems fictional, the windows do at least provide physical evidence, unlike most of the ghost stories that pub landlords tell and regulars have embroidered for generations.

LUDDENDEN: *THE LORD NELSON*

Luddenden: A646 Calder valley road to Luddenden Foot. At traffic lights turn uphill to Luddenden. Pass Kershaw House; fork left at Lord Nelson sign.

Once there were five pubs in the village; now just one survives, the Lord Nelson, formerly the White Swan. It was renamed after the battle of Trafalgar. Above the door is a plaque of the Admiral and the building's date, 1634 (with the 4 reversed), which makes it the oldest of the pubs in Luddenden. The pub and the church have an unusual date reversal: the Lord Nelson of 1634 and the church of 1814, when the opposite might have been expected.

Within, the pub has the customary three rooms: bar, lounge and games room. In the bar is a huge fireplace recently rediscovered after having been walled up for

The plaque of Admiral Nelson showing the date of the building.

many years. Also revealed was a priest's hole connected by means of a tunnel behind the lounge wall to the churchyard opposite, where the tunnel end was closed off after its likely need as an escape route was over. Because of alterations upstairs the fireplace can no longer be used for its original purpose; it now houses the pub piano!

On the wall by the bar is a quote by Branwell Brontë referring to the Lord Nelson: 'I would rather give my hand than undergo again the malignant yet cold debauchery which too often marked my conduct there.'

He was a regular at the Lord Nelson when he was a booking clerk in Luddenden Foot station and had a favourite seat at the corner of the bar. In 1776 a library was established in

The inviting exterior of the Lord Nelson.

The bar at the Lord Nelson.

an upper room as the result of a bequest of his book collection by a former vicar. Members were required to be of good behaviour and were fined for swearing or drunkenness: Branwell's drinking habits were notorious, so his membership of the library must have been precarious. Although the Lord Nelson's library served the village well, the public library service eventually replaced it.

The nineteenth century brought many changes to the way cities and towns were governed. It is unlikely that when Parliament approved rules governing mayor-making that villages the size of Luddenden were uppermost in the minds of the legislators.

Yet in 1861 the licensees of the Lord Nelson and their regulars said to each other 'Why not?' So it was that a new tradition was born. It lapsed as such things do, but is very much alive today. The election of the mayor of Luddenden is a community event, when the Lord Nelson is full and crowds spill over into the forecourt and the churchyard: too many for the new mayor to pay for drinks all round as the old custom decreed!

The unusual foundation of a library, the election of a mayor and the discovery of a priest's hole give the pub a special character; it should come as no surprise to learn that it has a ghost as well. Ghosts happen often at old pubs, usually turning beer taps off and causing pictures to fall from walls; at the Lord Nelson the licensee has to turn his taps back on weekly, and has a presence in the bar. A new activity has been the piano in the old fireplace sounding musical notes twice in one evening, convincing even the sceptics.

So steep are the hillsides at Luddenden that houses seem to be anchored on the slopes with two storeys on the front of the buildings and four at the back. Originally the village cottages were clustered by the bridge over Luddenden Brook; the sound of the water is very noticeable outside the pub and gives Luddenden its name – 'loud waters'. In medieval times people in and around the village were handloom weavers or raised sheep, but woollen mills were built in the valley to use water power. In 1842 a huge mill was built at Oats Royd between Luddenden and Booth, the first to use steam power.

Like so many Yorkshire hillside villages, Luddenden lacked good roads; in medieval times a track led from Halifax and Midgley to Luddenden and went on its lonely way to Burnley in Lancashire. It was called the Long Causeway. In 1820 New Road was built, bypassing Luddenden's ancient, narrow streets and allowing the passage of coal to Murgatroyd's Mill at Oats Royd from Luddenden Foot in the Calder Valley.

MARSDEN: *TUNNEL END INN*

Tunnel End Inn: A62 Huddersfield – Oldham and Manchester. At Marsden follow sign for station (car park). Cross railway bridge, turn left on to Reddisher road. Pub half mile on right.

There is a strange mystery and excitement about a long dark tunnel, and not just for little boys. Where does it go? What is at the other end? How long does the journey take? Why and how was it built? The questions are endless. So a pub set at a tunnel end and taking its name from it has a unique attraction.

True, the Tunnel End Inn was called The Junction until 1989; reopened in 2002 under its new name, it is enjoying a new lease of life. It was built in the eighteenth century and until recently would have had a competitor (even closer to the tunnel) called the Waters Edge, now closed. Both would have been well placed for the business that came with the construction of the new transport system that was to link the canal networks of Yorkshire and Lancashire.

First came the canal tunnel, the longest and highest in Britain; the canal itself had seventy-four locks. Next came the railways: three Standedge tunnels were completed, but only the third, with two tracks opened in 1894, is used today, carrying the line from Huddersfield along the Colne valley to Marsden, through the Pennines and on to Manchester. Both canal and railway were vital to Marsden in their day to allow the development of the local textile industry.

Today tourism is of great importance. The countryside, popularised by *The Last of the Summer Wine*, is beautiful and unspoilt. The Marsden Moor Estate of 5,685 acres of moorland is in the care of the National Trust and supports large numbers of moorland birds. Go by train to Marsden station, or leave the car at the National

Renamed in 2002, the eighteenth-century Junction pub is now the Tunnel End Inn.

The tunnel was built without a towpath, so the boats had to be 'legged' through by the men who lay on their backs and 'walked' the roof of the tunnel with their feet. They must have been overjoyed to see daylight here.

Trust visitor centre next to the station and walk on to the Tunnel End Inn. As their publicity says, this must be one of the few pubs whose clientele can come by road, canal, rail, foot, bike, or even horseback; there are still old tethering points outside for horses.

Just below the pub is the Standedge Visitor Centre where narrowboat trips into the 3¼-mile tunnel can be booked. By the side of the canal tunnel entrance watch the trains and hear them sounding their warning before plunging into the darkness of the railway tunnel.

A notice-board near the moorings for the narrowboats advertises the fantastic food at the pub. This is not an exaggeration: try a steak and ale pie, or a meat and potato pie, or even treacle sponge and custard, all home made. More and more visitors, including many National Trust members, are calling at the pub for drinks, coffee, or meals, especially the Sunday roast. Gary and Bev Earnshaw have received an award by Huddersfield and District CAMRA as Spring Pub of the Season 2003. They have three non-smoking rooms and a meeting room, all in traditional style.

Walking onward: beyond the Tunnel End Inn, follow the beck. The road narrows until a mile or so further on it ceases to be a highway; a public footpath leads on to the moors with walks in all directions, including a ramblers' route back to the quayside at the end of the tunnel. The walk gives the firm feeling that Foggy, Clegg and Compo have been around here, especially the sight of the magnificent packhorse bridge called Close Gate Bridge. The track over here would have taken packhorse teams across the moor to Littleborough.

Marsden itself has a delightful Cuckoo Day celebration every April. This is based on a legend that way back in the past Marsden folk tried to ensure that the cuckoo, which arrived with the spring sunshine, could be made to stay longer. They thought they could do this by building a wall round it. As a recent Cuckoo Day programme explains, 'It were nobbut just wun course too low'.

NUN MONKTON: *THE ALICE HAWTHORN*

Nun Monkton: A1M north to J47, then A59 York road. In about 5 miles turn left (dead end road).

Measured against the vastness of the Beningborough Hall estate across the river Ouse, the 18-acre village green at Nun Monkton seems only modest, although it is one of the largest in England. Most of the houses surrounding the green have grazing rights on it and the pond is home for ducks that appear to lay their eggs in whichever garden takes their fancy.

Looking across the green at the opposite end from the pond is the Alice Hawthorn. The pub together with its handsome wall sign harmonises well with its neighbours that fringe the green: the village layout has changed little since Domesday times. Its early name was Monechtone, its origins Anglo-Saxon; the pub

Nun Monkton's tranquil village green and pond.

Jaunty umbrellas outside the Alice Hawthorn offer a summer welcome.

was formerly the Blue Bell, having taken its present name, allegedly that of the owner's mistress, from a famous racehorse of the 1840s.

Alice Hawthorn was a winner for the first time at Northallerton in 1841 and in her career won 50½ races (one dead heat) from a total of 69 run. Her honours list including four Gold Cups was enormous and she continued her success after retiring to stud when she produced Thornaby, winner of the 1860 Derby.

Scenically there can be few pubs to match the Alice Hawthorn. At the point where the river Ouse turns sharply north it is joined by the Nidd; turning right out of the pub, an avenue leads towards the river, first reaching St Mary's Church.

The church was founded as a chapel for a priory of Benedictine nuns – hence Nun Monkton – in the twelfth century; no visitor should go to the Alice Hawthorn without also visiting the church, the surviving part of that nunnery chapel. The chapel's east end was demolished following the Dissolution of the Monasteries, but what remains is of great beauty.

The west door has three beautiful zig-zag decorated orders of arches and five colonettes. Above is a fine gable with left and right niches, one having a weathered statue. Inside there are arcades high up in the nave, all delicately decorated. The east wall, restored in 1873, contains three lancet windows by Morris & Co., including angels playing musical instruments by William Morris himself. The colours are, as always, pure and clear. These windows are considered the finest stained glass in West Yorkshire.

Next to the church is the gracious house known as the Priory; round the corner of the walled garden a gentle walk leads down to the banks of the two rivers.

Perfection may be an impossible dream, but Nun Monkton is as near as most of us can hope to find.

OSWALDKIRK: *MALT SHOVEL*

Oswaldkirk: From York B1363 Helmsley road to junction with B1257.

Very much part of the landscape of the Hambleton Hills, Oswaldkirk lies at the foot of the high tableland that overlooks the Vale of York. The high ground to the north of Oswaldkirk that shelters the village continues below towards Gilling East and then York, some 15 miles away. Ampleforth College is very close, with its fine church designed by Sir Giles Gilbert Scott.

Originally built in 1610 as the local manor house, the Malt Shovel has been in use as a pub for perhaps 300 years. The street frontage is plain and unremarkable, but its garden front is a total surprise and is the result of a rebuilding in the fashionable classical style in the early eighteenth century. Inside, the ground-floor layout of rooms off a wide central hallway shows that this was indeed a smart and important residence in its early days, and there is an original, beautifully made staircase. The Malt Shovel owes its name to brewing its own ale in the mid-

The Malt Shovel at Oswaldkirk.

The bar with landlord ready to serve.

The impressive staircase at the Malt Shovel.

The former brewhouse at the Malt Shovel.

nineteenth century, and the malt house and brewhouse were most likely the out-buildings that can still be seen today.

The Bamber family here had three sons in about 1890; one of them died suddenly aged five. His mother refused to accept his death and kept his body in a bedroom for some weeks before he was eventually buried. His ghost is said to haunt the pub. It is alleged to manifest itself in what is now the ladies' toilet!

The village is named after its parish church, which is of Saxon origin and is dedicated to St Oswald, once King of Northumbria following his victory over Cadwalla at the battle of Hexham in AD 634. He sent to Iona for missionaries to convert his kingdom to Christianity and they settled on the island of Lindisfarne. It was here that St Aidan and later St Cuthbert served their faith tirelessly. Like them, Oswald was canonised and has always been revered, particularly in the north.

RIBBLEHEAD: *THE STATION INN*

Ribblehead: A65 Leeds–Skipton–Settle. Turn right at river bridge in Settle on to B6479. Or A65 to Ingleton, then take B6255, Or take Settle–Carlisle train to Ribblehead.

There is a story about a man from Texas, where everything is larger than anywhere else, on his first visit to New York. His host took him to see the Empire State Building. Looking up, unimpressed, the Texan reacted with 'So what?' Those of us on our first visit to Ribblehead would seach for very different words: the over-used

The Station Inn and Whernside.

'awesome' comes to mind. Looking at the viaduct, perhaps 'Why did they even *think* of doing it?'

What a challenge this was! In all 72 miles of track had to be laid between Settle and Carlisle, requiring twenty major viaducts – of which Ribblehead is the most impressive – and fourteen tunnels.

Arriving by road at the crossroads below Ribblehead from Ingleton or Settle, the only visible places of shelter are the Station Inn, the Bunk House next door and a cluster of buildings at Ribblehead station. Beyond the pub is wild and unforgiving country dominated by the huge mass of Whernside, one of the famous 'Three Peaks'. The Midland Company's decision to build the railway through to Scotland here seems incredible, yet to the Victorians anything was possible – even the twenty-four arch viaduct that spans Batty Moss behind the Station Inn. Little imagination is needed to picture the hardship, especially in winter, endured by the workers; the wind speeds are phenomenal, accentuated by the height of the viaduct, 105ft.

The Station Inn, originally the Railway Inn, was built at about the same time as the viaduct, which was completed in 1875. The original licence was for a pub and farm, the first landlord being John Kilburn, who was also the local schoolmaster. He must have seen many of his pupils as customers at the pub in later years, and no doubt watched over their habits and behaviour. In due course his son Tom took over the licence.

Over the years changes to the Station Inn have been made; the building that was once a barn has been converted from farm to pub, and farmland was sold. If you are looking for a pub with a difference, here is one. Among its many differences and advantages it boasts a cast-iron solid fuel-burning stove, a comforting feature when bad weather, be it strong winds, rain or even snow, makes an unexpected appearance to the dismay of walkers. There is a comfortable bunk house, the only one discovered in researching this book. The curved bar has a discreet and unusual notice to its right: 'A Loo with a View'. And what a view it is, shared, of course, with the pub's other rear windows across to Whernside, 2,419ft in height.

The flat area towards Whernside across which the viaduct stretches to reach the Blea Moor tunnel was home to over 2,000 workers and their families while the southern part of the Settle–Carlisle railway was being built. They were housed in shanty towns, in conditions that can hardly be imagined, with names such as Belgravia and Jerusalem. The cost of the enterprise was heavy, both financial and human; in Chapel-le-Dale church over 200 lie buried, victims of accidents and of a smallpox epidemic.

The story of one accident displayed in the pub is that of Tapping George. He was a mason working on the tiers supporting the viaduct arches. One evening in January 1874 one of the hollow tiers was waiting to be filled with rubble when George was swept down into the depths by a gust of wind. His cries for help must have been drowned by the wind and his companions thought him dead from the fall, so

The dining room.

A place with a difference, and a ghost with a difference.

A train passing over the viaduct. The views must have been stunning.

nothing was done. The next day rubble was poured in on top of George who, it is now believed, had lain injured all night tapping with his hammer – desperately trying to attract help. He lies there today still seeking help, his tapping clearly heard by Three Peak walkers as they pass under the seventh arch of the viaduct. Ribblehead is a place with a difference, and certainly has a ghost with a difference.

Just a few steps across the road from the pub is Ribblehead station. Do go, but not before you sample one of the Station Inn's delicious (and filling) meals.

Even if you are not a train watcher, there is an excellent and well-stocked visitor centre in the station building. The arrival of a train, usually bringing and picking up walkers, is an event in itself. So far from the rest of the world, an indicator sign at the head of the train that says 'Leeds' gives an unusually reassuring feeling.

So much at Ribblehead is unusual and memorable that, as they say at the Station Inn, you will be planning your return visit before you leave.

RIPON: *UNICORN HOTEL*

Ripon: A61 north from Leeds.

The Unicorn Hotel was originally a timbered building, rebuilt in brick in the eighteenth century. We know that it was in existence in 1626 from legal papers that were signed and dated 'at the sign of the Unicorn in Ripon'.

The introduction of the unicorn as a supporter of coats of arms dates from 1603 when James VI of Scotland became James I of England. We know that he visited Ripon in 1617. The importance of the Unicorn Hotel to the city is well illustrated through its use by the Corporation for meetings in the seventeenth and eighteenth centuries when a new town hall was being built. The Unicorn became busier than ever, taking over a neighbouring shop and enlarging the premises to provide refreshment for coach passengers and a change of horses. The stabling was extensive and up to fifty horses were available.

Ripon had a considerable commercial business, with horse-drawn carriers fetching and carrying goods all over Yorkshire, even to and from Manchester and London. The Royal Mail between London and Glasgow called at the Unicorn each day and night and there were stage coach routes throughout the north and beyond. The 'Telegraph' was the outstanding coach, travelling between Newcastle and London, a journey of 300 miles, which it covered in thirty-six hours. Among its important stops was the Unicorn at Ripon.

Like the Golden Fleece at Thirsk, business continued in spite of the coming of the railways; passengers were taken to and from the station by the Unicorn's own transport. That overnight guests were important can be measured by the twenty-four bedrooms that were available. Familiar to travellers visiting the Unicorn in the mid-eighteenth century was 'Old Boots', Tom Crudd, whose responsibility it was to take a pair of slippers for their comfort and remove their boots. His 'Mr Punch'

The Unicorn Hotel at Ripon.

The plaque on the obelisk listing the duties of the wakeman.

features, with a massive nose and chin, allowed him to perform the trick of holding a coin between them. It was excellent entertainment for them and a good little earner for him.

The Unicorn Hotel's position on the Market Place means that it has always overlooked the major activities in Ripon and particularly on the market itself. Guests would have seen and heard the Ripon hornblower going about his nightly duty of blowing his horn at each corner of the Market Cross. The cross has been replaced by a 90ft obelisk, but the well-preserved tradition of horn-blowing goes back to Anglo-Saxon times. Indeed, the original Saxon horn still exists today.

In charge of the hornblower and responsible for maintaining law and order was the wakeman, or watchman; the sounding of the horn and the curfew signalled the 'setting of the watch'. The Wakeman's House, half timbered and dating from the fourteenth century, stands facing the Market Square, and the Town Hall nearby carries the city motto, 'Except ye Lord keep ye Cittie, ye Wakeman Waketh in vain'. Ripon's symbol is, of course, a horn.

RIPPONDEN: *OLD BRIDGE INN*

Ripponden: 5 miles SW of Sowerby Bridge on A58 to Rochdale.

It is generally believed that the Roman route from Chester to York passed over Blackstone Edge on the Yorkshire/Lancashire border. The track was a skilfully paved and channelled roadway of which a length survives today. Travellers would have come down the Yorkshire side into the Ryburn valley, then forded the river Ryburn, where a packhorse bridge was later built. In early days the place name was Brigroyd (the clearing by the bridge); today it is Ripponden.

Standing on the modern bridge that carries the B6113 road over the river and looking down it is easy to see why the Old Bridge Inn close to the packhorse bridge was always important. Just across the river is St Bartholomew's Church.

The pub is held to be one of Yorkshire's oldest – possibly *the* oldest, based upon a document of 1313 which records the existence of a bridge there. Antiquarians argue that the inn came later, in spite of the blue plaque on the front wall. What is also in dispute is whether it was originally a monastic hostel serving religious travellers. In the lower bar is a cross cut into the stonework, but whether this is a pilgrim's cross or a mason's mark is a matter of opinion. Certainly a monster beam, also in the lower bar, tells of great age. A curious stone figure, age uncertain, in the back of the chimney breast may have been brought in from elsewhere.

The long one-storeyed part of the building is the oldest and for many years the interior was open to the roof. Local historians love to tell of the restoration work done in 1882, when examination of a sample of lime from the wall revealed over 250 layers of whitewash! It was the house of Richard Hirstwood according to an eighteenth-century curate at Ripponden, but a flooding in 1722 destroyed most of the local records. The pub's name was the Waterloo for a time following Napoleon's defeat in 1815.

As is so often the case, the pub was not only a social centre, but a meeting place for charity trustees and other representatives. Auctions would have been held there and all the usual pub games. In an alcove on the left of the entrance a small plaque marks the meeting place of the Pork Pie Appreciation Society, formed over twenty years ago.

Old Bridge Inn, Ripponden.

A group of friends who had been exercising at a health club decided to go for a drink and a chat afterwards: the Old Bridge Inn was the nearest pub. One of the group brought pork pies to go with the drinks. As time passed the quality of the various pie-makers' products became an abiding interest and the Pork Pie Appreciation Society was born. Meeting every Saturday night (the only exception allowed was when Christmas Day fell on a Saturday) for a drink and pie tasting, the society decided to organise a pork pie championship in 1991, and this has been repeated annually ever since.

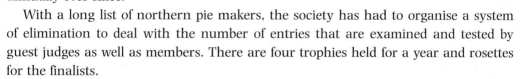

With a long list of northern pie makers, the society has had to organise a system of elimination to deal with the number of entries that are examined and tested by guest judges as well as members. There are four trophies held for a year and rosettes for the finalists.

The expertise built up over the years is considerable. The President Kevin Booth has been quoted as saying that to deserve an award a pie must be pretty, have nice pink meat, jelly round the sides and well-cooked pastry. Of course, it must smell porky. Judging a pie may not be a game of skill or chance as such, but the members enjoy the menu and the winner of the championship must find it good for business. Visitors to the society on a Saturday night are always made welcome, true to the tradition of a village pub.

Tradition is important, too, on the first weekend in September, when the Sowerby Bridge Rushbearing procession ends at Ripponden. After the presentation of rushes at St Bartholomew's Church, the Old Bridge plays a full part in all the celebrations that follow.

ROYDHOUSE: *THREE ACRES*

Roydhouse: A629 Huddersfield–Sheffield, to Kirkburton. Fork left B6116. At Shelley continue up hill, then turn left towards TV mast. Pub on left.

In their welcome to guests at the Three Acres the Truelove family say, 'Head for the Emley TV mast and you will find us nearby'. With such a landmark, finding the Three Acres is certainly one of the easiest journeys to plan: after all, the mast is sited on a high point of the countryside. It overlooks the Holme valley and has fine views, as the Three Acres does of distant Pennine moorland.

Roydhouse, the address of the Three Acres, is one of the tiny hamlets on the fringe of Shelley, an ancient village where handloom cottage weaving went on for centuries; most outside employment was in agriculture or mining.

Roydhouse – or 'house in a clearing' – stands high up over Shelley and today has a sprinkling of stone cottages and farms. It is ancient too; early records show that for a long period it was a place of residence of respectable families. Evidence of a change of land ownership in 1324 arises from a charter relating to Nicholas de Schellay and records land in 'le Roides'. Even earlier a charter was granted to Peter de Scheluelay 'de le Rodis in villa de Scheluelay with all pastures and woods'. Shelley and Roydhouse clearly existed then.

Modern conveniences like pressing a light switch or turning a tap came slowly to Roydhouse; today's grandparents easily remember the van that delivered paraffin for lighting and heating and the two little back-room shops, one selling sweets, the other a variety of convenience items. A long walk to Shelley was an unattractive proposition in bad weather, particularly in the big snow of 1947 when 'every able-bodied shovel' tackled the huge snowdrifts. In those days most of the men worked at one or other of the two pits on either side of Roydhouse, or on one of the five working farms. The largest of these was Roydhouse Farm, which had its own private chapel: when this was closed a new chapel was built at Emley in 1909, only for it to be destroyed by the fall of the TV mast.

Now, with most of the contours ironed out, the outcroppings of coal behind the village cottages can hardly be seen; in spite of the danger of collapse these were worked by local people picking coal. Inevitably there was a tragic accident and picking ceased.

A drovers' inn, known as The Plough, with an attached brewhouse served by its own lined well, was the first pub at Roydhouse; a second, long since closed, was called the Cherry Tree. The deeds for the present roadside inn and restaurant date back to 1807. It was renamed the Three Acres from the attached land shortly before

The Three Acres, Roydhouse.

The pub sign with Emley TV mast in the background.

it was purchased by the Truelove family in 1969. That was the year of a very severe winter when the first Emley Moor TV mast collapsed. Goodbye landmark! Just as the new modern tower replaced the earlier fallen one, Derrick and Muriel Truelove began the transformation of the Three Acres, building up the catering side while maintaining a thriving bar trade.

Their son Neil Truelove, together with Brian Orme, the head chef, continued the development of the Three Acres from the early 1970s, adding bedrooms in the 1980s. Today there are twenty en-suite bedrooms and an excellent wine cellar; there is seating for 150 diners.

Among its many achievements, the Three Acres received *Yorkshire Life* magazine Food and Wine Awards 2002–2003, Dining Pub of the Year for Leeds and West Yorkshire. This provided a valuable wider recognition of the Three Acres' reputation for outstanding food.

A newcomer to the Three Acres entering from the car park may well be surprised to make a first acquaintance with The Grocer, an acclaimed delicatessen, offering a wide range of quality produce, which was added in 1999. Something unusual is always to be found there. As ever, new ideas emerge at the Three Acres, such as an extension to the restaurant, which opened in June 2004.

SALTERSGATE: *SALTERSGATE INN*

Saltersgate: From Pickering A169 towards Whitby.

There can be few more colourful settings than the heather moorland that seems to stretch for ever behind the Saltersgate Inn. As the traveller comes out of a sharp bend midway between Pickering and Whitby close to the spectacular Hole of Horcum, there it is in all its glory.

A halfway house before the days of the motor car when roads were little more than tracks, the inn must have been a welcome refuge in winter from the cruel east winds across the moor. A shelter it surely was, and notorious it certainly became as a store for smuggled salt, which was heavily taxed in the eighteenth century.

Fishermen from Whitby needed supplies to salt their fish, and where better to go for untaxed and illegal salt than the remote Saltersgate Inn? Here are the ingredients of the Saltersgate Inn legend, 'The fire that never goes out'.

The Saltersgate Inn.

One night in 1796 a Customs and Excise officer making enquiries was murdered by smugglers, who buried his corpse under the hearthstone. To ensure that his body was never found, a tale involving the Devil was concocted. He was said to have burst into the inn one night and to have threatened the regulars with damnation. To pacify him they offered him a seat by the fire, then pushed him into the flames.

Should the fire ever go out, the story says that the Devil will escape and terrorise the countryside, so even now it continues to burn day and night whatever the time of year and whatever the weather. A sort of insurance policy!

SAXTON: *GREYHOUND AND CROOKED BILLET*

Saxton: A1M north to J45, A64 east to Tadcaster, then A162 south. At Towton fork right on B1217.

One of the smallest pubs in Yorkshire, the Greyhound recalls the earliest days when brewsters' homes were open to the public. A view of the flower-decorated Greyhound with the church beyond is a reminder of the link between the pub and the church: the pub at Saxton was once a twelfth-century barn and still has its heavy beams and flagged floors. There is one tiny bar where the regulars always gather, a small snug and a games room.

The Greyhound at Saxton, with the church in the background.

In Saxton churchyard there is a tomb chest of Lord Dacre, Lancastrian leader killed at the Battle of Towton. The inscription reads 'Here lies Ralph, Lord of Dacre and Gilsland. A true soldier valiant in battle in the service of Henry VI who died on Palm Sunday 29 March 1461, on whose soul have mercy.' At this vital battle of the Wars of the Roses, probably the bloodiest ever fought on English soil, some 30,000 died, resulting in victory for the Yorkists. A memorial cross stands a mile or so away by the side of the road to Towton.

Only a short walk across the fields west of the Greyhound is the Crooked Billet, the probable Yorkist headquarters in 1461; certainly a pub has stood on the site for 600 years.

Tradition has it that Richard Neville, Earl of Warwick, stayed here at the time of the Battle of Towton and the coat of arms hanging outside the pub contains elements of the arms of the Nevilles. The prominent silver diagonal cross is said to have been called the 'crossed sticks' locally, hence the Crooked Billet.

The Cock Beck runs beside the road across from the pub. It was against the beck, further downstream, at that time too deep to ford, that the Lancastrian army was trapped, hammered by a gale force wind and blinded by snow driven into their faces. The Cock Beck was said to have run red for twenty-four hours. Many of the dead were buried in mass graves in the middle of the field opposite the Crooked Billet.

The lonely little church of St Mary, Lead, across the road from
the Crooked Billet, is of fourteenth-century origin. The village it
served has been abandoned and lost; very occasional services are
held in the church. Although St Mary's did not figure in the
Battle of Towton itself, the peaceful fields where sheep now graze
became a burial ground for many Lancastrians, and it is thought
that the wounded were given shelter in the church.

Above: The impressive tomb of Lord Dacre is in Saxton
churchyard just north-east of the church; you are likely to find
both red and white roses within the enclosure to commemorate
him and the dead of two armies. *Right:* Also regularly decorated
with red and white roses is the stone cross by the side of the road
high up overlooking the battlefield. It is usually known as
Dacre's Cross, but he is thought to have been killed a short
distance away downhill from the cross. Its significance is as a
memorial to the many who paid the ultimate price.

The Crooked Billet at Saxton.

Also in the field is the small church of St Mary near the deserted medieval village of Lead, but there is no confirmation of its link with the conflict on Palm Sunday 1461.

Time has long since removed the visible signs of battle and the Cock Beck is now only a narrow stream. Memorials remain, though, and many visitors follow battlefield walks, setting out from the Greyhound or the Crooked Billet.

SCAPEGOAT HILL: *SCAPE HOUSE INN*

Scapegoat Hill: From Huddersfield A640 Rochdale road, 1 mile beyond Outlane cross M62 on bridge, climb to crossroads, left at standing stone.

On this high lonely tableland with its distant views of moorland features such as Stoodley Pike above Todmorden and the monument on Castle Hill at Almondbury, it is an unlikely spot to find a village, over 1,200ft above sea level. That it was once a textile settlement is just as surprising, with a working population of handloom weavers and every home having at least one loom.

Scape House Inn stands on the corner of High Street and School Road, looking out across the valley towards Linthwaite; its style is much like that of the neighbouring cottages that line the street. The only building of any size is close by:

The Scape House Inn at Scapegoat Hill.

Guidepost of 1756.

The Band Hall.

the Baptist chapel of 1899. Past the chapel and wide stretches of heather beyond lie the bare crossroads with a standing stone carrying the date 1756, originally serving as a guide and a distance post. Although local buses wind their way up slowly from the valley today, life must have been lonely in the past and travel hazardous.

Scapegoat Hill is a fine example of an isolated community that has had to provide its own leisure activities. Some small organisations might have been home-based, but even these would need the pub for annual meetings. The variety of societies and clubs is astonishing, but it is not surprising that (in textile areas particularly) many villages had their own brass bands. The enthusiasm that inspired Brighouse and Rastrick, or Black Dyke at Queensbury, was certainly to be found in small villages elsewhere.

In the nineteenth century, when there was a Scape-goat Brass Band, they would have had their annual meeting at the pub that was then called the New Inn. Unlikely as it may seem today, they had their own Band Hall, now a private house.

One elderly resident of the village tells the tall story of the severe winter of 1956, when snowstorms trapped the bandsmen in the Band Hall for four days. He believes that they only survived thanks to the large stock of beer at the hall, adding swiftly that he was not a bandsman himself!

Until well after the Second World War villagers had to depend on their own water supply from the Spring Head Well. Housewives had to carry buckets to it on Halifax Road, where spring water flowed into a stone trough; according to the oldest residents it never ran dry, however severe the drought. A tap by the trough remains today and cool water still runs.

As for the village name, a local tombstone with the date 1817 shows it as Slip Cote Hill; a variation, Slipcoat Hill, is mentioned in rental documents of 1701. Why the name changed to Scapegoat after 1817 is a matter of surmise. Was it the loneliness of the place that reminded incoming weaver families of the biblical story of the scapegoat released into the wilderness as an atonement?

Perhaps the origin of the word slipcoat itself, which was once the local name for cream cheese, may have referred to a place used for cattle grazing. Who knows?

SETTLE: *ROYAL OAK HOTEL*

Settle: From Leeds A65 via Skipton. From Lancashire M6 J31 then A59 to Gisburn. There join A682/A65 to Settle.

Tuesday is Market Day in Settle, attracting many visitors from the surrounding area as well as large numbers of local people. As in Chester, where Welsh accents are heard as often as those of Cheshire, so in Settle. Lancastrians mingle with the

The Royal Oak Hotel at Settle.

The Royal Oak's main rooms that look out on the Market Place owe their sixteenth-century atmosphere to the alterations carried out in the 1930s. The fireplace's extensive carving and panelling have created a strong feeling of antiquity.

Yorkshire folk, their accents clearly distinguishing one from the other, a reminder of how close the county border is.

The Royal Oak looks out on to the Market Place, so the bar and dining room there have the same mixture of voices as outside on the streets. Quite apart from the weekly market, Settle has always been a popular town for visitors. Walkers come this way for the Three Peaks: Whernside, Ingleborough and Pen-y-Ghent, the Forest of Bowland and Ribblesdale. The Settle–Carlisle Railway, with 72 miles of spectacular landscape, twenty viaducts and fourteen tunnels, is compulsive viewing for the railway and engineering enthusiast.

The bar of the Royal Oak leaves customers in little doubt as to where they should order their food. The wainscoting makes a warm and mellow welcome.

A plaque on the front of the Royal Oak reading 'RMBC 1686' was probably placed there by the Cookeson family who were property owners here, and confirms that the pub is one of the oldest in Settle. The pub sign is a reminder of the escape of Charles II from Cromwell's troopers searching for him after the battle of Worcester in 1651, when he hid in the famous oak tree at Boscobel. The Royal Oak sign is one of the most popular in the country, showing loyalty and affection to Charles after the Restoration of the Monarchy in 1660. The king died in 1685, so the house was built soon afterwards; was it *just* a coincidence that the pub was named the Royal Oak?

In spite of a rebuild in about 1720, the Royal Oak needed enlargement to deal with the increasing needs of eighteenth-century horse-drawn traffic. The Keighley–Kendal turnpike in the second half of the century created a need for horses to be permanently stabled and ready to replace tired teams; feeding and shelter for horses, drivers and passengers were essential and made excellent business.

The coming of the motor car and yet more traffic in the twentieth century made an updating and extension of the premises needful again, but now it was brewery capital that made it possible. As a result the traditional English inn has emerged after a number of alterations; the dining room was formerly part of the pub yard where horses were stabled, and the downstairs rooms were opened up to provide more space. Seen from the entrance, oak panelling, a substantial bar and a fine staircase with a hanging carpet are the Royal Oak's trademarks as a comfortable call-in refreshment stop or as a residential inn offering bed and board.

The Royal Oak claims to have had a number of 'in the news' guests over the years, such as Sir Malcolm Campbell and Sir Mortimer Wheeler, but its place in Settle life is firmly based on the welcome it gives to all visitors, including this author.

SHEPLEY: *CASK & SPINDLE*

Shepley: A629 Huddersfield–Penistone road.

Looking downhill from the railway arch and the Cask & Spindle on Abbey Road, the skyline is dominated by the Emley TV mast. A fearsome turn in the road at the bottom of the hill marks entry to Shepley's neighbour Shelley. If the similarity of names confuses you, do not despair. You are in Yorkshire after all: what about Skipton and Shipton, or Collingham and Cottingham? There are others, of course, as well as several Scholes.

Shepley's name is very descriptive: 'meadow of the sheep'. Before woollen mills were built all along the valley from Penistone to Huddersfield flocks of sheep would have grazed and provided fleeces for the textile hand workers. When the mills did come fine worsted became Shepley's speciality, together with tailoring using locally produced cloth. Some thirty outhouses to Shepley cottages became nineteenth-century workshops and places of employment.

Sadly, the textile mills have gone, like the brewery and maltings that produced a fine beer using pure spring water. The Cask & Spindle's name is a reminder of both industries and is the last of a line of pub names from the past. Oddly, one of the clauses in the deeds of the building requires it to remain as a safe house in emergencies for the nearby railway, so unsurprisingly it was at first the Railway Inn.

The Cask & Spindle, Shepley.

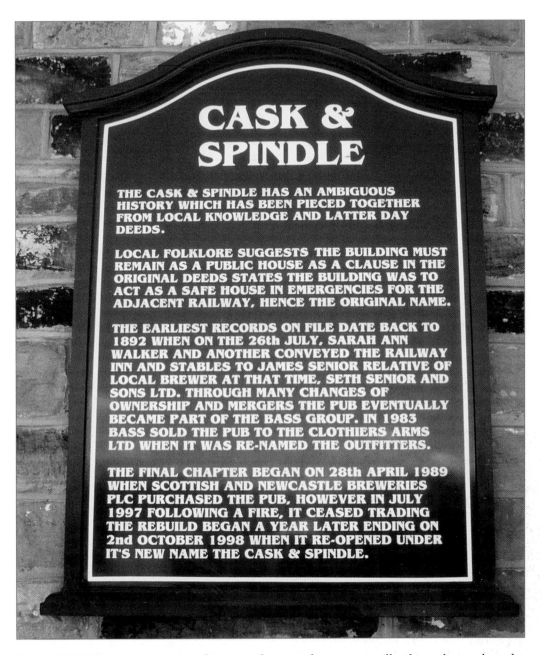

CASK & SPINDLE

THE CASK & SPINDLE HAS AN AMBIGUOUS HISTORY WHICH HAS BEEN PIECED TOGETHER FROM LOCAL KNOWLEDGE AND LATTER DAY DEEDS.

LOCAL FOLKLORE SUGGESTS THE BUILDING MUST REMAIN AS A PUBLIC HOUSE AS A CLAUSE IN THE ORIGINAL DEEDS STATES THE BUILDING WAS TO ACT AS A SAFE HOUSE IN EMERGENCIES FOR THE ADJACENT RAILWAY, HENCE THE ORIGINAL NAME.

THE EARLIEST RECORDS ON FILE DATE BACK TO 1892 WHEN ON THE 26th JULY, SARAH ANN WALKER AND ANOTHER CONVEYED THE RAILWAY INN AND STABLES TO JAMES SENIOR RELATIVE OF LOCAL BREWER AT THAT TIME, SETH SENIOR AND SONS LTD. THROUGH MANY CHANGES OF OWNERSHIP AND MERGERS THE PUB EVENTUALLY BECAME PART OF THE BASS GROUP. IN 1983 BASS SOLD THE PUB TO THE CLOTHIERS ARMS LTD WHEN IT WAS RE-NAMED THE OUTFITTERS.

THE FINAL CHAPTER BEGAN ON 28th APRIL 1989 WHEN SCOTTISH AND NEWCASTLE BREWERIES PLC PURCHASED THE PUB, HOWEVER IN JULY 1997 FOLLOWING A FIRE, IT CEASED TRADING THE REBUILD BEGAN A YEAR LATER ENDING ON 2nd OCTOBER 1998 WHEN IT RE-OPENED UNDER IT'S NEW NAME THE CASK & SPINDLE.

From 1892 there were many changes of ownership; eventually the pub was bought by the Clothiers' Arms Ltd in 1893 when it was renamed the Outfitters. In 1997 after a fire it ceased trading; a rebuild followed and it reopened in October 1998 under its new name, the Cask & Spindle.

Shepley has a railway station on the Huddersfield to Sheffield route and the Cask & Spindle is on the Penistone Line Pub Trail list, conveniently located about halfway between Huddersfield and Penistone. A short distance away from the pub is an unusual conversion of one of the line's signal boxes into a three-bedroomed house. By 2003 only one other similar conversion had been permitted – in Wales.

SHIBDEN HALL, HALIFAX: *CRISPIN INN*

Shibden Hall: Lister's Road, Halifax, off A58 Leeds road.

When is a pub not a pub? Look no further than Shibden Hall, Halifax. In the care of Calderdale Metropolitan Borough Council Museums and Arts Department, Shibden Hall is a 1420 half-timbered house once owned by the Lister family. Anne Lister, the last member of the family to live here, died in 1840, having made great alterations to the house and grounds to create the appearance of a baronial hall. It was gifted to the people of Halifax in 1923.

In its role as a folk museum, the hall has seventeenth-century furniture and a large barn. Around the courtyard are craft workshops such as those of cloggers, saddlers and coopers, and also the Crispin Inn – with the purpose of showing aspects of the way of life in the district.

Sad to say, there are no drinks on sale at the Crispin Inn, which is a re-creation containing the bar from the original pub of that name which once stood close to Halifax parish church. St Crispin is the patron saint of cobblers, passing into our history through the Battle of Agincourt which was fought on St Crispin's Day 1415. Remember Laurence Olivier as Henry V? One small pub at Ashover in Derbyshire took the Crispin name in honour of the men of the village who fought at Agincourt and returned safely, so it is truly an ancient title.

Shibden Hall.

The interior of the Crispin Inn.

Coopering equipment at Shibden Hall, together with casks and metal hoops used to pull the staves together to prevent leaking and to shape the casks.

Crispin Inn, with Knur and Spell implements.

The Crispin Inn bar at Shibden Hall has all the fittings in use some 200 years ago, including beer pumps, kegs and glass bottles. Of special interest is a working example of one of the strangest pub games played locally, called Knur and Spell. The equipment consists of the spell, a kind of spring trap which throws a ball of wood or porcelain – the knur – into the air when released. The player taps the spell with his pommel, or club, to release the spring, then tries to drive the airborne knur as far as possible. Competitions – even championships – took place on fields close to pubs with teams playing for serious money, up to £100.

Wooden pegs were driven into the ground at 20 yard intervals (a score of yards) to simplify and measure distances; the record seems to have been set in 1899, when Joe Machin of Sheffield recorded 15 score of yards and 14ft (314ft).

After the Second World War there were only a few older competitors left and there was little interest among possible younger successors. A revival in the 1960s at the Spring Rock Inn, Greetland, came to nothing in spite of sponsorship from Samuel Webster, the Halifax brewers, and others.

The last championship is believed to have been at Stainland, between Halifax and Huddersfield, in 1979. Those were the days when life was simpler and our excitement came from real village activities rather than contrived and impossible thrills on the TV screen.

SHIBDEN: *SHIBDEN MILL INN*

Shibden: A58 Halifax to Leeds road to Stump Cross crossroads. Turn to Shibden; in about ½ mile fork left down hill.

If you enjoy a sunny May day, the sound of lambs and the colours of wallflowers, aubretia and lilac, then the Shibden valley is the place for you. Shibden seems greener in spring sunshine than anywhere else, perhaps the reason for Shibden's early alternative names: Chepdene, or Schepedene, the 'valley of sheep'. There, wool was provided for the local textile industry, which tells us much about the way of life for early dwellers in Shibden.

The first record of a pub's existence at Shibden Mill is in August 1890 when the buildings there were sold to the Halifax brewers, Websters; the first landlord was a Mr E.C. Sutherland Walker. The mill itself burned down in 1859, so some sort of new business was needed.

Things have moved on considerably since then. Although the present pub buildings – originally separate cottages – have been opened up, creating rooms of different sizes and character, they share features such as flagged floors and timbering, including low beams and ceilings. Beware the entrance door if you are over 6ft tall! One large fireplace has been removed, increasing the open space between rooms, but an interesting fireplace at one end of the ground floor has the date 1643 in the stonework.

Shibden Mill Inn.

The interior, with its ground floor lounge furnishings.

It is upstairs in the restaurant that spectacular timbered roofs have been exposed, creating a unique atmosphere. Upstairs or down, here is dining with history.

Further recent extensions along Shibden Mill Fold and a refurbishment have provided comfortable hotel accommodation, transforming the early pub of 1890 into a twenty-first-century restaurant with rooms. Residents here have a wide variety of visitor attractions available, not least the beautiful valley walks; just across the A58 Leeds road is Shibden Hall and its park.

The remains of stonework on the mill site show where the mill wheel once turned, while the stream that fed power still runs by the edge of the main car park; sadly the mill pond has gone. Old prints show leisure boats on it, but it was drained some time after the pub was set up, probably to prevent water draining into nearby mines. It is now filled in and used as an extension to the car park.

The mill was originally a manorial corn mill dating from at least 1308. Corn and oats were milled and local people were required to have their milling done here. In the eighteenth century the mill was owned by the Lister family; their ownership lasted for over a hundred years. It is interesting that when Thomas and George Bottomley took it over, probably in 1845, they operated the mill for worsted spinning. An invoice of 1853 confirms this, but as we know the mill was destroyed by fire in 1859.

Until 1883 May Day was celebrated with a maypole at the inn, where the garden has been built and where tables and chairs have been set out for warm weather use. The twenty-first century really came to Shibden Mill Inn when ITV chose it for a cameo role in *The Royal*, a spin-off of *Heartbeat*. When the programme was first aired on 22 June 2003 regulars had no difficulty recognising their local.

STAINFORTH: *CRAVEN HEIFER*

Stainforth: A65 to Settle, then B6479 at the river bridge.

Of the huge variety of pub signs, the Craven Heifer is one of the most unusual, depending as it does on a fragment of agricultural history in the Craven district, thus confining examples of the Craven Heifer sign to Yorkshire and mainly to Craven, the Skipton area, although there are a few other examples, including at Bradford.

This enormous beast was born in 1807; by March 1811 and still growing, the heifer was 5ft 2in at the shoulder and weighed over a ton. At that weight it compared favourably with one of the massive Shires used to pull brewers' drays.

The Craven Heifer pub stands next to the little stone-arched bridge over the beck at Stainforth, north-west of Settle in the heart of Ribblesdale. Along the river Ribble and close to the road up the dale from Settle are former textile mills; the traffic along this route in early days was that of the packhorse going between Lancashire and the north-east of England. There is no doubt that the Craven Heifer's customers at Stainforth two hundred years ago were the packhorse traders seeking rest and refreshment. The landlord believes that even earlier monks used the building for food and shelter.

Today it is tourists who are the focus of the Craven Heifer's business. This is outstanding walking country; just up the road is Horton-in-Ribblesdale, the traditional start point for the Three Peaks Challenge, a 23-mile route over Pen-y-Ghent, Whernside and Ingleborough. This is strictly not for the faint-hearted, but the views of the peaks from the comfort of a car ensure admiration for the stamina and courage of the competitors.

The pub is small and full of character. Its smoking room on the front here carries the old title the Vault, with the restaurant facing across the entrance passage. The main bar and snug stretch across the back of the building; above the fireplace is a framed print of the Craven Heifer with a dedication to the Duke of Devonshire, on whose property at Bolton Abbey the great animal was raised by the Revd William Carr.

Life at the Craven Heifer must have been unpredictable, as an early landlord felt compelled to post a notice listing the rules of the inn. Dated 1786, these included:

The friendly interior of the Craven Heifer.

The packhorse bridge over the Ribble.

'Flintlocks, Cudgels, Daggers and Swords to be handed to the innkeeper for safe custody'; 'Bed for the night: one shilling'; 'Stabling for horse: four pence'.

A more recent notice in the form of a brass plaque says: 'His Royal Highness the Prince of Wales launched "The pub is the hub" guide at the Craven Heifer, Stainforth Monday 17th December 2001'.

The friendly pub ghost is known in the village as Tacksy (spelling dubious and various). He wanders around at night opening doors and passing the kitchen windows without triggering the exterior security lights. Unusually, the landlord knows the ghost's favourite drink: Martini Rosso. There is rarely an order for this, but the level of drink in the bottle always falls quickly – much more so than for other varieties. There is no evaporation and no drips under the upturned bottle. Who is the secret drinker? Tacksy, of course.

Only the barman has seen a 'being'; at the time he knew nothing about any ghost here. One quiet afternoon when the pub was empty he suddenly became aware of a customer behind him with his hands in the air. This person was dressed in a huntsman's pink coat buttoned up to the neck. The barman turned round for a glass and the customer disappeared. He was nowhere to be found.

An ancient and beautiful packhorse bridge spans the river Ribble nearby. It can be reached by crossing the B6479 and is well worth the walk down the steep lane – and even the climb back!

STANBURY: *OLD SILENT INN*

Stanbury: A629 from Keighley. Haworth; Inn beyond Stanbury village.

Once named the Eagle, the building dates back over 400 years. Its isolated position on the lonely road from Haworth to Laneshaw Bridge with the windswept Haworth Moors of the Brontës for company gives it a special character. Looking across the valley a few scattered dwellings at Oldfield can be picked out, and it is hard to believe that only a few miles away lies industrial Keighley.

There were home brewed ales on sale here for many years, a business that was combined with farming. The house still has its oak-beamed rooms, small windows, thick walls and traditional fireplaces, all of which create atmosphere and encourage legend. One story features Bonnie Prince Charlie who, it is said, was hidden here when on the run in the eighteenth century, his safety being secured by the silence of the locals. There is no historical evidence for this, but the story does provide a reason for the pub's change of name.

The Old Silent Inn is listed in *Haunted Inns of England*. A former landlady in cloak and hood used to go out on to the moor at night to feed roaming cats and called them by ringing a bell. Today there are those who say they have heard the bell. Imagination, perhaps, but at six o'clock on a recent Monday morning just such a

The Old Silent Inn, Stanbury.

bell was heard by a team of investigators who spent the night at the inn to try to record any ghostly activity.

Using monitoring equipment they recorded several distinct knocks on a locked door, and sounds as if someone was trying to enter the room. Inside the room voices, especially that of a child, and a dog barking were heard, and on opening up later objects placed there had been moved. To the team's amazement a large handprint was found on a towel at the bottom of the bed. In the bar a stool tipped on to two legs and refused to lower itself.

The Old Silent Inn was the most active place the team had investigated, and a further visit may be able to confirm these and other unexplained happenings.

TADCASTER: *ANGEL & WHITE HORSE AND SAMUEL SMITH, THE OLD BREWERY*

Tadcaster: A64 towards York then A659 1½ miles east of A1M junction.

The first written record of a brewhouse in Tadcaster comes from the tax return of 1341, but there is a firm belief that it was the Romans who sank wells here and discovered the brewing qualities of the local water. They certainly built a military station called Calcaria by a crossing over the river Wharfe and controlled the road to the great fortress at York: Eboracum. It is entirely likely that one of the buildings at Tadcaster would have provided legionaries with a place for drinking and recreation.

The Angel & White Horse, Tadcaster.

The White Horse painting.

Samuel Smith's stables.

Hogshead, one of the current team of Shires. You may see them grazing in a field by the A64 close to the bridge over the river at Tadcaster.

Evidence may be thin, but we can safely conclude that in the centuries that followed the Roman retreat in AD 420 alehouses served the people of Tadcaster and travellers who passed through the town. As elsewhere, it was coaching business that brought prosperity in the eighteenth century, especially to pubs on important roads. The Angel, along with the White Horse next door, catered for many of the passengers and mail coaches calling at Tadcaster on their way to York, Hull, Leeds and Manchester.

The special quality of water drawn from this limestone area made local beers so popular that Tadcaster is today a brewing town: the evidence for that is in the air of the town. Modern brewing began in 1758 when a brewery was set up behind the White Horse, but within a hundred years the railways came, bringing unwelcome change. The brewery behind the White Horse became a victim of change and was bought up by John Smith, today a household name. A family disagreement after John Smith's death led to one of his brothers leaving the old brewery and establishing a brewery of his own, while the other brother Samuel's family remained at the old brewery, the name that is still used.

The Angel closed in the mid-nineteenth century, the White Horse being renamed the Londesborough Arms. In 1976 the Londesborough was converted into Samuel Smith's brewery offices, easily recognisable with a handsome four-column porch. The Angel was renovated, incorporating some parts of the White Horse, and reopened under its new name Angel & White Horse – with a double hanging sign of an angel blowing a trumpet above the white horse.

The windows of the pub still look on to the main street along which coaches used to pass before swinging into the courtyard. In a place of honour in the bar above the fireplace is a large painting of a white horse and across the courtyard are the Samuel Smith stables, home to six massive Shires, around 8ft tall and weighing upwards of a ton. From their stable homes, with names such as Hogshead and Mild, fed, groomed and immaculately turned out, these Shires still pull a dray and make a few local deliveries for the Old Brewery.

The company prides itself on brewing at Yorkshire's oldest brewery and uses traditional methods and stone Yorkshire fermenting squares, with the yeast being of the same strain since the beginning of the twentieth century. Tradition is of great importance to Samuel Smith, and it is seen in the employment of their own coopers to make and repair all their own casks, the only brewery in Britain to do so.

THIRSK: *GOLDEN FLEECE*

Thirsk: A1M then A169 Teeside road, or A61 from Leeds via Ripon.

The pub sign here is a specially attractive one, enhancing the Golden Fleece's already elegant exterior facing the Market Place (there is a similar sign in Pavement, York, opposite the end of the Shambles). It tells allcomers that this was a

The Golden Fleece, Thirsk.

business pub where wool business would be done and where wool men would meet. The Golden Fleece dates from late Tudor or early Stuart times and there is a rainhead dated 1791. Like many other important inns it had other functions: in this instance it was the Land Registry in the early eighteenth century for the then North Riding.

The Fleece and its neighbour the Three Tuns shared the coach traffic through Thirsk, and by 1823 seven coaches a day called at Thirsk. In 1791 the pub was enlarged to handle the growing traffic, becoming the best known coaching house between York and Darlington. As a result there were always fifty to sixty horses here and part of the extensive stables remain today in the rear courtyard.

When the railway came to Thirsk many feared a serious loss of business as coaches disappeared, but the Golden Fleece continued to prosper as railway passengers still needed food and accommodation. There was plenty of local trade and Thirsk has always been a shopping centre for a wide country area. There is always competition for parking spaces on the Market Place today, but parking discs from local shops have made this much easier.

Across the Market Place from the Golden Fleece, the street at the left-hand corner is Kirkgate, which leads to St Mary's Church, one of Yorkshire's finest in the Gothic style; nearby is Georgian Thirsk Hall.

No. 23 Kirkgate is probably the most visited house in Thirsk, now known as 'The World of James Herriot' and formerly the veterinary surgery of Alf Wight, as Herriot was in real life. It has been opened as a museum which presents the house as it once looked as a veterinary practice.

TRIANGLE: *THE TRIANGLE INN*

Triangle: M62 to J26 then A58 to Halifax. Continue A58 towards Rochdale via Sowerby Bridge. Car park faces the pub.

There is nothing quite like the English countryside for names that puzzle and origins that astonish. The Triangle Inn is one of these, as the village was named for the pub, not the other way round as might be expected.

It all began to happen when, in 1735, a turnpike trust was formed to remedy the appalling state of the road from Halifax to Rochdale which was often impassable, particularly in winter.

Where the Triangle Inn now stands, between Sowerby Bridge and Ripponden, the new road passed through a hamlet then known as Stansfield Pond, with a row of houses facing Stansfield Mill Lane, which led to a textile mill by the river Ryburn. The Stansfield family were important land and mill owners and their factory provided employment for a large number of people, resulting in the growth of population locally.

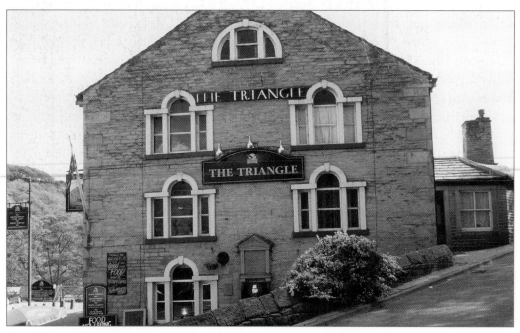

The Triangle, Halifax.

The former stables at the Triangle.

The new turnpike changed everything, not least the name Stansfield Pond, as the road created a triangle between itself and a side road leading uphill to Mill Bank. On this small piece of land a pub was built in 1760; it was registered as a coaching inn a few years later, becoming known as the Triangle. By 1777 the hamlet itself began to be commonly known as Triangle.

Stage coaches continued to call at the Triangle until 1886, a year after the opening of the branch railway line from Sowerby Bridge to Rishworth. This closed to passenger traffic in 1929, although it remained open for freight until 1952. The Stansfield Mill closed in the 1970s. There were even trams when Triangle was the terminus in this direction from Halifax.

The pub is a survivor of the several pubs at Triangle in the nineteenth century and is large enough to be a well-used coaching inn, having an extensive bar area and lounge across the front of the building and a games room at the rear. At the left-hand end of the bar are two attractive arch-roofed rooms, handsomely converted from the stables, once a necessity for a coaching inn.

On the wall at the Sowerby Bridge end of the building is something quite rare for a pub: a war memorial for the twenty-five men of the district who fell in the First World War. This was unveiled in 1920 and has recently been restored.

It is at Triangle that the Sowerby Bridge rushbearing procession halts for a rest and a performance of morris dancing before setting out on the last lap of the 9-mile route that ends at Ripponden on Sunday afternoon.

WARLEY: THE MAYPOLE INN

Warley: Off A646 Barnsley Road at Cote Hill, Halifax. Sowerby Bridge: A58 between Halifax and Rochdale.

The Maypole pub dates back well over 200 years, although in earlier times it was known as the Horns. The building was originally a farm and the farmer probably also ran the ale house. In 1773 it was owned by Joseph Farrar, who owned the gaol and smithy next door too.

There is a huge mural on the gable end showing the maypole that stood outside. In 1900 this was replaced by a drinking fountain, as the May Day celebrations had become too rowdy.

In spite of the loss of the maypole, the pub is still very much part of local tradition. On the first Saturday in September the annual Rushbearing Festival begins at St John's Church, Warley, followed by the parade, which has its first stop at the Maypole, a rest break for the marchers, who take refeshment there.

Music, morris dancing and all sorts of traditional merrymaking go on outside the Maypole before the rush cart is taken off on the way to its stops at Sowerby Bridge. There, celebrations take place at various venues including the canal basin. Sunday's route goes steeply uphill to Sowerby village, St Peter's Church and the aptly named

The Maypole Inn, Warley.

Rushcart pub for refreshment. Out into the country, the procession then goes to Cottonstones for the presentation of rushes at the beautiful little church there, then to Saw Hill and Triangle before the end of the festival is marked by a Songs of Praise at St Bartholomew's, Ripponden.

The ancient festival of rushbearing is a deep-rooted tradition, recalling the annual changing of the rushes once used to cover stone or earth floors of churches. While the rushes helped to keep worshippers' feet warm, their annual replacement with freshly cut rushes was not just a practical need. It also had a strong symbolism: 'Out with the old' and 'On with the fresh and new'.

In the past this annual event was marked by a festival and holiday, but had fallen into disuse until revived at Sowerby Bridge near Halifax for the Queen's Silver Jubilee in 1977. The two-day festival held at the beginning of September is now well established and attracts crowds from a wide area.

A traditional rushbearing cart, its pointed roof thatched with 500 plaited bundles of rushes cut from the waterside on the moors, is the centrepiece of the 9-mile two-day procession. The cart takes ten days to prepare and decorate; its weight of nearly a ton needs sixty 'pullers' to reach hill tops and ten 'brakemen' in the rear to cope with the steep downhill parts of the route. The pullers' costume is as traditional as the festival itself: clogs, Panama hats, white shirts and black trousers. The brakemen in similar costumes wear rubber-soled clogs to help them in their hair-raising job of preventing a runaway.

The rushbearing cart.

The rushbearing procession.

Over the years the festival has grown and grown. All are aware of the religious aspect of the event: it is not just an excuse for a pub crawl even though there are stops for refreshments, marked in the programme with a tankard symbol at several pubs along the route of the procession.

There is also a programme of family entertainment: several teams of morris dancers, mummers, village galas, brass bands and a variety of street activities, with children playing a full part.

WATH IN NIDDERDALE: *THE SPORTSMAN'S ARMS*

Wath: either from Harrogate A61 north to Ripley roundabout then B6165 to Pateley Bridge; at bridge turn to Wath. Or from Skipton B6265 to Threshfield and Grassington. Continue B6265 to Pateley Bridge; turn to Wath.

Set among trees and green hill slopes, the Sportsman's Arms can only be reached by negotiating a steep packhorse bridge over the river Nidd, thought to have been built by monks of Fountains Abbey. Nearby are the stone cottages of the village, but the overwhelming feeling is one of peace and quiet far from the noisy activity of the rest of the world.

Popular with lovers of the countryside and for relaxing breaks, the Sportsman's Arms is ideally placed only a mile away from Gouthwaite Reservoir, a sanctuary for birdlife of all kinds, especially waterfowl. Two miles long, it is a man-made lake, part of the course of the river Nidd, and it makes a considerable contribution to water supplies in Yorkshire.

A typical lunch hour in the bar area of the Sportsman's Arms will have customers en route to or from bird watching, dale walking or just having a break from motoring along the dale. The pub was purpose-built in about 1890 when rooms were large and comfortable; such is the restaurant, while more intimate is the residents' lounge, used also for non-residents waiting for tables at lunch and dinner. Prominent and unusual are the huge round wall clocks, once used on local railway stations that are now closed. Flowers are a speciality; Thursdays are 'flower days', when visitors can expect to see new displays being prepared by the domestic staff.

Sportsman's Arms, Wath in Nidderdale.

The former station house at Wath.

Very close to the pub stands a large stone house with a slightly familiar look – and a very beautiful garden. Familiar, perhaps, because it was once the Wath station house. Across the road the track bed of the former Nidd Valley Light Railway can clearly be seen on its way up the dale to the other stations at Ramsgill and Lofthouse. It was the building of the reservoirs in Nidderdale that created the need for a transport system for materials and workers. It opened in 1907 with four trains a day and continued for passengers until 1929, by which time buses proved more economical. When the last reservoir was finished in 1936 the Nidd Valley Light Railway closed altogether – a sad loss.

The delightful house sign.

A delightful reminder of this history is on the address board of the former station house close to the Sportsman's Arms, which in addition to the house name shows a small steam train in action, making smoke as in the old days. It is worth walking the short distance further down the lane to look at the packhorse bridge and lean over the low parapet to watch the waters of the Nidd running down to Pateley Bridge.

WENTWORTH: *GEORGE & DRAGON*

Wentworth: M1 J36 to Hoyland Common, then turn left on the B6090.

What makes a village and a pub unusual? Wentworth and the George & Dragon provide the answers. Two versions of the Domesday entry can be quoted – perhaps there are two of most things at Wentworth – 'Winteworth' and 'Winteworde', so the settlement is an ancient one. Wentworth's oldest building (now ruined) is the 'old' church of 1235 where it was believed Thomas Wentworth, Earl of Strafford, beheaded in 1641, is buried. This has been disputed, although the family chapel has a number of Wentworth tombs. The 'new' church is dated 1875.

The George & Dragon was built in the early seventeenth century as a farmstead. Occupying a central position on Main Street, it provided space on what is now the pub car park for the local market and annual fair. It is likely that ale was sold then, but the village was still small and the pub would have needed business from travellers to add to that from villagers to make a living, together with the farm.

Wentworth is still an estate village, although the 10th Earl Fitzwilliam died in 1979. Fortunately he had already set up the Fitzwilliam Wentworth Amenity Trust to help maintain the quality of life and property in the village. Wentworth

The George & Dragon, Wentworth.

An interior scene at the George & Dragon.

Woodhouse, England's largest house, really two eighteenth-century houses in one, one facing east, the other west, lies on the fringe of the village; its huge park was over 9 miles round. Its building symbolised great wealth and power, but it is no longer home to the family of the builder, Thomas Watson Wentworth, who became first Marquess of Rockingham.

The George & Dragon received its first full pub licence in 1804, when we know that the innkeeper was Robert Pepper. There must have been additional land for its service as a court house. The large grassy area at the rear today is very inviting on warm days and evenings for outdoor refreshments and a play area for children. By the side of the front car park the extension to the main rooms forms an L-shape and shows the George & Dragon to have been both large and important.

The bar stretches across the front of the main building with further seating upstairs and an intimate 'snug' towards the rear. This has a preserved ancient entry round the corner of the bar that reveals the enormous thickness of the walls as well as its age. By the main entrance are the Best Pub awards: four of them in the last few years.

It is a rewarding experience to explore Wentworth village. The 'old' church has already been mentioned; the second and 'new' one of 1875 has fine stone vaulting and tracery. The 195ft spire is a reminder of South Dalton in East Yorkshire (see page 26); both churches were designed by J.L. Pearson. In Clayfields Lane is a windmill, built in 1745 and long since converted to a private residential building.

Another delightful conversion is named Paradise Square; this was once a farmhouse and yard. The house itself is at the top of the Square, while the outbuildings on either side stretching down to the road are now cottages, with the space in the centre transformed into an attractive garden. Nearby is the Mechanics' Institute of 1835, built many years before anything similar was considered in larger Rotherham.

At the top of the village at the Gun Park is Wentworth Brewery, which began production in 1999 – yet another unexpected feature of Wentworth.

To underscore the unusual character of Wentworth, be prepared for a surprise if you happen to arrive at the George & Dragon in advance of (say) 11.30 a.m., a common opening time. The door will surely be open from 10 o'clock, and breakfast – what a breakfast – will be available until noon. If you choose the famous and popular Walkers' Breakfast, the Wentworth Experience will be yours. It is one not to be missed.

WEST WITTON: *FOX & HOUNDS*

West Witton: A1 to Leeming Bar, then A684 west via Leyburn.

In the days when vast areas of countryside were in the ownership of monasteries, it was the monks who exploited the fruits of the land, whether this was the lead from mines, or wool from sheep grazing in Wensleydale. West Witton was part of territory in the hands of Jervaulx Abbey; the Fox & Hounds and adjoining houses were believed to have been named Cathedral Hall. Today the Fox & Hounds' next-door neighbour has a prominent Cathedral Hall house name over the door.

The Fox & Hounds has a date of about 1400 and there are suggestions of religious connections. During the excavation of a 7ft thick wall a past landlord unearthed a tiny chamber which he was convinced was a place of penance used by those who lived there. The chamber was so small that it would only allow one person to kneel inside with bent shoulders.

A link with Wensley church before the Reformation is possible, and a stained glass window in the vestry of St Bartholomew's Church near the pub shows the arms of the abbots of Jervaulx: three shells on a blue background. It is likely that this was removed at the Dissolution of the Monasteries from a private chapel at Chantry on the side of Pen Hill, above West Witton.

The Fox & Hounds, West Witton.

The large fireplace at the Fox & Hounds.

It is Pen Hill which overlooks the sunny patio dining area at the back of the Fox & Hounds. Steps go down to a long corridor leading to the bar, where a large stone fireplace remains as a dividing wall to create two rooms at the front. At the back is a separate dining room where the massive fireplace still has its original bread oven. The pub's cellar has been hewn out of solid rock.

One of those festivals that are a feature of village life in England takes place at West Witton and, naturally, the Fox & Hounds is involved. Called West Witton Feast, it is held on the weekend nearest to St Bartholomew's Day, 24 August. The Whitby Penny Hedge, the Midgley Pace Egg Play, the Ripon Feast of St Wilfrid and, of course, the Sowerby Bridge Rushbearing are other Yorkshire examples.

At West Witton, in addition to a Cottage Show, tea and an evening Fell Race, there is the extraordinary Burning of Bartle. Because of the name given to this ancient custom celebrated on St Bartholomew's Day, some people give it a religious significance. The contrary view is that it cannot represent the burning of St Bartholomew, a much revered saint; more likely, the argument goes, Bartle was a criminal – a thief perhaps – who was warned to stay away from the village. Ignoring the warning, Owd Bartle, as he is often called, was found in the village and chased out, his life ended by burning.

At 10 p.m. young men of the village form up in procession past the Fox & Hounds and, carrying a straw effigy of Bartle, follow the traditional route to Grisgill (or Grass Gill) where Bartle is burned. The rallying cry is well remembered:

> At Penhill crags he tore his rags
> At Hunters Thorn he blew his horn
> At Capple Bank Stee happened a misfortune
> and he broke his knee
> At Grisgill Beck he broke his neck
> At Wadham's End he couldn't fend
> At Grisgill End we made his end.
> SHOUT, BOYS, SHOUT!

At which point the crowd cheer, and finally at Grisgill End Bartle is set on fire and favourite old songs are sung. The pub does good business; whoever Owd Bartle was, there is something in it for the Fox and Hounds.

The pub has a handsome Fox and Hounds sign, although there is no connection with a hunt. This name was adopted between 1870 and 1880, the Punch Bowl having been used earlier. Fortunately the pub is familiarly known as The Fox, which distinguishes it from the Fox and Hounds not far away at West Burton.

YORK: *BLACK SWAN*

From railway station follow ring road anti-clockwise. At Castle, continue ring road (here called Foss Islands Road) along river Foss. At Layerthorpe Bridge cross into Peaseholme Green. Pub on left opposite St Anthony's Hall.

Ancient English cities often gained an unwelcome reputation for having more pubs than there were days in the year. Small many of them may have been, but the result was that in crowded city streets pubs would have had several close neighbours all in competition with each other.

In York, this was the case. Although today there are many attractive nineteenth-century pubs, others reflect the city's medieval past. One of these, the Black Swan, is strikingly timber framed and dates back to the late sixteenth century, or perhaps even before. Standing close to Layerthorpe Bridge over the river Foss (not the Ouse), it faces St Anthony's Hall, one of York's guildhalls.

There are twin gables fronting the street, with a central block having a jettied, or overhanging, first floor, such a feature of the Shambles and other ancient York streets. Modern extensions have been constructed at the rear. Fine seventeenth-century open well stairs lead to the first floor, where there is painting on the walls to create an illusion of panelling – a so-called 'trompe l'oeil' with a laurel leaf frieze and painted overmantel. Upstairs wall paintings, now almost faded out of existence, carried a religious message, and there is a tradition that Margaret Clitheroe, the Catholic martyr whose shrine is in the Shambles, was arrested in the house.

Before becoming an inn in about 1715, this was the house of the Bowes family. Successive generations were Lord Mayors of York; in 1545 Sir Martin Bowes was

The Black Swan.

The painted panelling in the Black Swan.

Lord Mayor of London and Treasurer of the Royal Mint. The house was occupied later by another Lord Mayor of York, Edward Thompson, whose daughter Henrietta was the mother of James Wolfe, the famous General Wolfe of Quebec. It was in Edward Thompson's time that further improvements to the house were made, and he was probably responsible for adding the open-work stairs. Although serving as a coaching inn for some time, the Black Swan declined and came close to dereliction. A recent restoration fortunately revived its fortunes as a pub and it is one of York's historic buildings.

YORK: *THE BLUE BELL*

Park and Ride No. 3 to Castle, or car to Castle car park. Continue on foot via Castlegate, turn right into Coppergate and Pavement. Pass Marks & Spencer and turn right into Fossgate (one-way traffic, narrow and congested).

In the *Travel Mail* Andrew Martin wrote, 'York: the best of the old – symbolised for me by the Blue Bell in Fossgate, the most accidentally perfect pub I know – has survived.'

Squeezed between a musical instrument shop and the Army & Navy Stores on crowded Fossgate, with double yellow lines running past its narrow frontage, the Blue Bell might appear to be a victim of its surroundings. Unlike the extraordinary columned entrance of 1911 to the former Electric Theatre nearby, now a furniture store, the Blue Bell does not assert itself. Neither does its glazed brick front compete with the beautiful coat of arms of the Gatehouse of the Merchant Adventurers' Hall lower down Fossgate.

Yet once inside the Blue Bell, its two modest rooms speak for themselves as something very special. The Edwardian interior remains entirely as it was after a refurbishment in 1903: a small bar at the front with nine beer pumps, and behind a glass screen the Smoke Room served through a hatch. This is a friendly, conversational room, small enough for an open fire to provide both warmth and intimacy. Throughout the Blue Bell ceilings and walls are of polished wood. The passage to the Smoke Room at the back also has a serving hatch, at one side of which

The Blue Bell, York.

is a folding seat that a latecomer would find useful on a busy day.

The clientele at the Blue Bell is as varied as any town pub is likely to be; what they have in common is that they know each other and have plenty to talk about. The rooms are small enough for drinkers to feel that they are in company with each other and with the bar staff. On a random Tuesday were two businessmen relaxing in their lunch hour and chatting at one table, another was in conversation at the bar, while the oldest 'regular' was in the corner finding his way into a hard-boiled egg, and this reporter was taking photographs. Nothing to shout about, perhaps, but a great deal to be thankful for: the Blue Bell's simplicity and its preservation are a credit to one family, the Robinsons. George, followed by his wife and then by his daughter Edith were licensees for much of the twentieth century. Mrs Edith Pinder was the last of that family and retired in 1992.

Ancient the Blue Bell is not, neither is it an architectural showpiece, nor does it tell of shadowy figures from the past, plotting or fighting around its walls. Yet it well deserves its place on the list of Yorkshire's historic pubs because it shows us simply and genuinely what an Edwardian interior was really like. This is history in its best sense – the history of ordinary people and their social environment.

YORK: *KING'S ARMS*

Park and Ride No. 3 to Castle, or car to Castle car park. Continue on foot from Tower Street by Castle taking Clifford Street past fire station. Turn left to King's Staithe and continue along river bank to King's Arms by Ouse Bridge.

Located just below the Ouse Bridge on what was once a busy commercial quay, the King's Arms is the only survivor of a number of inns that were a part of the history of the river front here. It began business in the 1780s. The building itself

The King's Arms, York.

probably goes back to the sixteenth century and is the oldest on King's Staithe; since then its appearance and name have changed. Timber framed in its early days, the King's Arms was later clad in brick; in the mid-nineteenth century it was called the Ouse Bridge Inn, reverting to the King's Arms in 1974.

Unusually, the pub has two different signs; that on the quayside shows Richard III, while his arms, supported by two white boars, hang on the side of the building round the corner at the bottom of King Street. This was one of the so-called Water Lanes leading down from Castlegate to the quayside, attracting in the past a disreputable clientele. Today the reputation of the King's Arms is very different. Looking down from the Ouse Bridge on a summer's day is to see crowds of tourists and locals enjoying the sunshine and an open air drink on the Staithe outside the pub. From here during the holiday season the Original Ghost Walk of York sets out every evening at 8 p.m. for a night of history and mystery.

The King's Arms' out of season reputation can be even more spectacular. It has been variously described as 'the famous pub that floods', 'York's most flooded pub' and even 'York's famous underwater pub'. Cumberland House, a handsome neighbour on the Staithe, had its main entrance built at the side, several feet higher than the quay itself. The King's Arms eventually felt compelled to move its entrance

FLOOD LEVELS
RECORDED AT
THIS INN

4·11·2000

5·1·1982

30·3·1947

30·12·1978

2·4·1940

11·12·1965

2·2·1995

6·10·1933

16·9·1931

Left: The upstairs cellar.
Above: The flood marker.

to the side nearer Ouse Bridge for the same reason: to allow entry when the river overflowed. The level of the Staithe had been raised in 1774, but flooding of the river since then has been so severe that the water has invaded the pub on numerous occasions, as well as bringing parts of York to a standstill.

This has meant that the 'cellar' of the King's Arms is upstairs, in a room where bodies of criminals hanged off the Ouse Bridge used to be displayed. Downstairs in the bar near the door is the famous marker that shows the height of the water there when floods have taken place over the years.

The present record was set on 4 November 2000, when the Ouse reached some 6ft above the bar floor, at least 11ft above the level of the quayside. As one of the regulars remarked, 'We thought it was time to leave.'

2. YORKSHIRE'S WOOLLEN PUBS

Ask any Yorkshire football fan where the Blades and the Minstermen play. Without hesitation the answer will be Sheffield and York: it is all a question of identity and loyalty.

So much of Yorkshire's social and industrial history has been bound up with wool that it came to represent a way of life. From the grazing of sheep for the fleece and the early cottage industry in hilltop villages to the huge mills in the river valleys and faraway markets, whole communities came to depend on wool. Identity and loyalty in the community and in 'their' pub became just as important as that of football supporters in the twenty-first century.

A day may come when some of the processes and jobs in the woollen industry are nothing but history. Future generations are likely to be totally baffled by cropping, for example, and wonder why the Croppers Arms was given its name.

Such is the importance of the woollen pubs that examples have been collected together and follow here, along with other buildings of woollen interest.

One of Yorkshire's most interesting and important woollen buildings is Halifax's Piece Hall. It was built in 1775 by Thomas Bradley to serve as a cloth market. It has over 300 rooms on the various levels where the cottage weavers from the surrounding district sold their handiwork. It now houses an open-air market; in the colonnades are shops, a café, an art gallery and Halifax Tourist Information Centre.

BARKISLAND: *THE FLEECE*

Ripponden Old Bank: A58 Sowerby Bridge to Rochdale road. At Ripponden turn left on B6113 over bridge.

Taking merchandise to market has always been important, often difficult and dangerous. Ripponden Old Bank, both long and steep, is one of the most

formidable routes that packhorse teams carrying woven cloth had to negotiate. It's no surprise then, to find a pub on the hill where the teams could stop for rest and refreshment before continuing south. It must have been with great relief that they paused at the Fleece.

Way below is Ripponden in the Ryburn valley and further distant is the Calder valley. Fine views are to be seen from the garden at the rear of the Fleece, although perhaps less appreciated by packhorse teams than by today's motorists or walkers. A few cottages face the pub across the road.

Although the date over the door is 1737, that just records when the pub was rebuilt following the seventeenth-century destruction by fire of an older building on the site. During its life the Fleece has been a farm and has accommodated an early friendly society; in every way it has been a typical country inn, developing to meet the needs of succeeding generations. When the Pennine turnpikes came into use, and the days of the packhorse were done, the Fleece became a coaching inn and served wheeled traffic.

Today's facilities were not available for eighteenth-century coach passengers, but with the M62 not far away the Fleece now offers a quiet and comfortable overnight stay with en-suite bedroom accommodation. Two connecting ground-floor rooms at front and back have bar service and beamed ceilings; first-floor seating is available as well as 'snug' table and chair space.

When they light one of the fires at the Fleece it is time to back off by several yards – a practical illustration of the pub's warm welcome.

The Fleece at Barkisland.

The property was rebuilt in 1737 after the much older original building was destroyed in a fire. It had a variety of uses before it became a pub.

CHICKENLEY: SPINNERS ARMS

Chickenley: M1 J40, then A638 Wakefield–Dewsbury Road.

One of the most unexpected features of the 'woollen' pubs in Yorkshire is that there are now so few. The industry has declined, of course, and with that decline has come a severe fall in employment in textiles. There may be little point any longer in names such as the Spinners Arms, or the Weavers, when no mills exist any more in their neighbourhoods. Certainly many pubs have changed their names, and closures have been all too common.

An example of a pub that disappeared was reported in the national press recently under the banner heading 'The historic pub lost by the Town Hall'. It seems that the White Lion in Stafford was taken down stone by stone in 1978 to allow for the building of a ring road. Put into storage pending a rebuild elsewhere, all the stones and timber have vanished. The local authority don't know where it is and would be grateful for any leads that would help to find it. Yet another example of the various explanations for vanishing pubs!

Chickenley's Spinners Arms is one of the few left with that name, and possibly it will soon be the sole survivor in the West Yorkshire woollen district. As part of Dewsbury, famous for its blankets and 'shoddy', Chickenley would have had many spinners living and working nearby. Originally a beer house, the Spinners in Chickenley Heath stands on the busy Wakefield road formerly lined with workers' terrace houses, now cleared. As the only building with bay windows, the pub is prominent in photographs from between the wars, especially with its signs at first-floor level.

Early records are sparse, but the Spinners Arms was in business in 1853. By 1869 it was owned by Bentley's Yorkshire Breweries Ltd of Woodlesford, Leeds. Village loyalty was particularly strong in the days when people had to make their own entertainment and the local pub was the place where most activities were based. The Spinners Arms had its own rugby football team, now sadly gone. Local rivalries must have produced other competitive activities such as darts, but only very long memories would be able to recall life at the Spinners.

The Spinners Arms, Chickenley.

HIGHTOWN, LIVERSEDGE: *SHEARS INN*

Shears, Hightown, Liversedge: M1 J40, A638 to Dewsbury. Turn right under railway arch. A638 to Heckmondwike. Turn left A649 Hightown, Liversedge.

Framed on the wall in the most prominent position in the bar of the Shears is *The Hartshead Ballad*. The first two verses run:

> I was as good a cropper
> As Liversedge did see
> Until the death of a neighbour's child
> From hunger maddened me.
>
> They took our living from us
> And put in machinery
> 'Til men who once walked quiet
> Grew crazed with misery.

Perhaps a lament would be a better title for the story of the tragic events that had their focus in this rather ordinary pub in 1812. The local shearmen or croppers used to meet in a clubroom over the front rooms on Saturday evenings, and it is their story that is enshrined at the Shears.

They were cloth finishers in the woollen industry using traditional methods to give a smooth finish to cloth, only to be threatened by the introduction of labour-saving machinery, principally Harmar's cropping frame at the end of the eighteenth century. Two local factory owners brought in the new cropping or shearing frame: William Horsfall at his Ottiwells Mill and William Cartwright of Rawfolds Mill at Liversedge.

Since the frame, tended by one workman, could do the work of ten hand croppers, the desperation of the men of the Spen valley facing the sack and starvation can well be imagined. It would be easy to understand how they were influenced by the so-called Luddites from Huddersfield and elsewhere into using violence. Encouraged by the success of attacks on mills elsewhere, croppers from Birstall, Cleckheaton, Gomersal and Heckmondwike formed a secret society based at the Shears. The landlord, while being well aware of the croppers' meetings, knew nothing of the conspiracy.

The first successful action by the croppers was an attack on a convoy bringing cropping frames over Hartshead Moor for William Cartwright. They then decided to attack Rawfolds Mill, but Cartwright had

The Shears Inn, Hightown.

prepared his defence, including members of the Cumberland militia. Met with gunfire and unable to break in, the Luddites had to withdraw with several wounded. Two were left dying. Their story is continued on page 150.

After the murder of William Horsfall the Luddite conspirators were rounded up, and sixty-six were tried at York for the three acts of violence: eighteen were hanged.

In an alcove near the *Hartshead Ballad* is a collection of items associated with the Luddite events: a pair of traditional shears and photographs of a shearing frame and of Enoch. Enoch Taylor of Marsden made cropping or shearing frames and Enoch was the name given to the great sledgehammer used to smash machinery: 'Enoch made them and Enoch shall break them'.

Also on display are the coats of arms of the Fitzwilliams and the Radcliffes. The Lord Fitzwilliam was Lord Lieutenant of the West Riding in 1798 and under his command the army was used to crush the Luddites. Joseph Radcliffe was appointed magistrate for Huddersfield; he was rewarded with a baronetcy following his interrogations which forced Luddite members to turn King's Evidence and resulted in the hangings.

In pride of place at the Shears is the impressive badge of the croppers for all to see. After the trial the Shears ceased to be the headquarters of the local Luddites, but continued to be what it had always been: an important feature of the locality's social life.

ROBERTTOWN, LIVERSEDGE: *STAR INN*

Roberttown: M1 J40, then A638 to Dewsbury and Heckmondwike. At A62 turn towards Huddersfield. Keep right for Roberttown.

Although the name of this pub has no connection with the woollen industry, it played a vital part in the tragedy of 12 April 1812, following the doomed attack by the Luddites and their followers on Rawfolds Mill the previous night (see pages 148–9).

In the knowledge that troops were looking for the conspirators, they became fugitives, desperate to avoid capture. The two so seriously wounded that their lives were in danger, Samuel Hartley (24) of Halifax and John Booth (19) of Huddersfield, were taken by the authorities first to the Yew Tree Inn, now a private residence called Headland Hall. This was originally a clothier's house of 1690. It seems that crowd trouble was feared, so Hartley and Booth were transferred to the Star Inn; their suffering must have been dreadful, considering the cruel journey from Rawfolds to hilltop Roberttown, then the move to the Star that followed. The landlord of the Star Inn was greatly concerned at the involvement of his pub in all this, as he had the reputation of keeping one of the most orderly houses in the district.

Both Hartley and Booth died within hours of their arrival at the Star, neither revealing any information to the authorities. A grim tale is repeated in all accounts of the night's happenings concerning the Revd Hammond Roberson, who visited the dying men. He was commonly believed to be anti-Luddite and it was alleged that his purpose in seeing them was to obtain information. The dying Booth is reported to have said to him, 'Can you keep a secret?' When the parson immediately said he could, Booth replied, 'So can I'. The deaths at the Star ended a short but very sad chapter of the Star's history.

Life at the Star had not always been like this. In happier times it was a popular venue for visitors to the annual Roberttown races that took place on Peep Green. The common land stretched some distance from the Star, and at one point the course crossed the main road; on one occasion the horses ran into a wagon and a jockey was killed, resulting in the races being replaced by a village fair.

The Star consists of two houses joined together on a sloping site. Originally the Star was built with a corner door, a common arrangement for local shops and pubs, and consisted of one room with a small bar in a recess facing the door. Stonework alterations show this, as they do along the side of the building where a bay window has gone, also an entrance door; there is now a modern stone porch. Inside, the extension into the lower level building made steps necessary into a second area with a large bar and a conservatory.

At one time there were stables at the rear, where the local chimneysweep kept his horse and cart and pigs were bred. Photographs from the 1920s show the pub with a large notice proclaiming 'Springwell Ales', which came from a former brewery at Heckmondwike.

The Star Inn at Roberttown, Liversedge.

Village life at Roberttown for generations depended on spinning and weaving. Curiously, in this predominantly woollen area, the late nineteenth century saw an 'invasion' of workers brought by John Wright to weave cotton at Roberttown. Cottages known as Cotton Row were built to house them, the workers being fed close by at Rattlecan Hall. This weaving went on until the Second World War.

Life has been hard at Roberttown, especially at the time of heavy unemployment in the nineteenth century. It is particularly sad that the events of April 1812 should have spilled over to Roberttown and the Star Inn.

HILLHOUSE: *THE SLUBBERS ARMS*

Hillhouse: From Huddersfield Ring Road take A641 Bradford road. At first lights turn left, The Slubbers opposite.

Since its opening in 1853 the pub's name has remained unchanged. It is believed to have been chosen because the then owner's son was a slubber. In the textile industry slubbing is the removal of knots of wool following the carding process. The Slubbers at Huddersfield is the only pub with that name in England, making it a unique part of the local industrial scene.

The intriguingly named Slubbers Arms.

The address of The Slubbers, 1 Halifax Old Road, shows the pub to be located at Hillhouse, at the start of an early route to Halifax. Looking from the traffic lights on Bradford Road, Huddersfield, today it is clear that this has always been an important crossroads where travellers leaving Huddersfield turned from the route to Brighouse and Bradford and climbed steeply to go over the top towards Elland and Halifax.

Within a few yards the roads divide, with The Slubbers standing on a sharply pointed junction created by the road pattern. The result is a door at the pub's 'sharp end' with the building widening towards the rear, where neighbouring property has been taken over as an extension. In the nineteenth century, when the pub was built in a congested area of workers' dwellings, it must have seemed a good location for business and a corner position of great potential. In Huddersfield's textile heyday there would have been six mills or so in the immediate vicinity, bringing in plenty of business for The Slubbers and other nearby pubs.

The bar today has some fine examples of textile items, a collection of ale jugs and bottles, reminiscences of the glory days of Huddersfield Town Football Club – indeed a massive display of what the licensee calls paraphernalia. A bona fide 1888 fire range is quite surrounded by textile industry photographs and posters, including 'Rules of the Mill' and 'Rules for the duties of an Overlooker'.

While the bar and snug are full to the ceiling with the collections, the games room at the 'sharp end' has quite a different atmosphere. There is no piped music at The Slubbers, but plenty of conversation. The pub was awarded the Winter Pub of the Season 2003 by the local branch of CAMRA, but whether there is any connection between the no music regime and the award must remain a personal point of view!

MARSH:
THE CROPPERS ARMS

Croppers Arms: M62 J23, A640 towards Huddersfield centre, or From Huddersfield A640 Rochdale Road. Pub ½ mile from town centre.

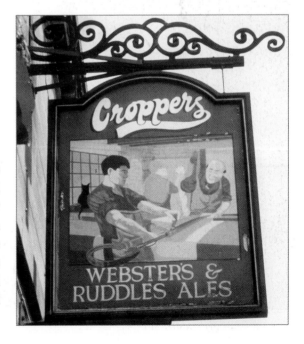

One of the finishing processes in the production of woollen cloth involved the hand raising of the nap, followed by the use of shears to ensure that the cloth had an even, smooth surface. The name Croppers Arms would appeal to the many textile workers in the Huddersfield area, especially the highly skilled hand croppers or shearmen in or near Marsh.

Exterior of the Croppers Arms.

The Croppers Arms contains some interesting pictures and memorabilia.

'Cropping' at the Tolson Memorial Museum, Huddersfield.

In the mid-nineteenth century it was a beer house with something of a bad reputation, and was eventually closed because of gambling on the premises. It appears to have been three cottages originally, although oddly it only has one cellar, which might argue that it was purpose-built as a pub. At the end of the century it was owned by the Wappy Spring Brewery, which used to stand in Lindley Moor Road by the side of the still-existing Wappy Spring pub.

When the licensee of the Imperial Hotel in Huddersfield calculated that a pub on Westbourne Road in Marsh would be a good proposition he was quite right, but the only way he could secure a licence there was by means of a transfer. He persuaded the magistrates to transfer his Imperial licence to the Croppers Arms in 1909 and took his chance. It turned out that he chose the right spot at the right time.

The location of the Croppers Arms on one of the main routes into Huddersfield and close to the town centre is certainly one of the factors in its success. Marsh itself was once a separate community, probably taking its name from common land on the boundary of the town of Huddersfield. Old maps show the land marked by a stone cross which has now disappeared. Today Marsh is very much a part of Huddersfield township, but retains an identity of its own. Certainly the pub has a large number of local regulars as well as many visitors from beyond Marsh. Evening bar meals are hugely popular and the present licensee has developed residential business by offering four en-suite rooms. Apart from the bar accommodation downstairs, there is a separate dining room.

Unlike many pubs these days, there have been very few changes of landlord: only five in the life of the Croppers Arms. Possibly not a world record, but as good as any recommendation a pub can have.

NETHERTHONG: CLOTHIERS ARMS

Netherthong: A616 Huddersfield –Sheffield to Honley, at Honley fork right A6024 towards Holmfirth, turn right at mill buildings on both sides of road, B6107, keep right in village for Clothiers.

From Berry Brow on the fringe of Huddersfield, a journey of 15 miles up the Holme Valley in the nineteenth century would have passed close by sixty woollen mills. So say the regulars at the Clothiers with some pride, although the great attraction of water power has long since gone and most of the mills have disappeared along, sadly, with very many jobs.

The pub takes its 'woollen' name from the men who were the organisers and financiers when industry was based in homes and every member of the family had a role in the work involved. In such a dispersed system there was a need for businessmen to supply the raw material – wool – to the many spinners, weavers and finishers, and then to market the product. These businessmen were known as clothiers and the pub's name confirms what is evident from the many mullioned upper windows of Netherthong's cottages, that it was a weaving village.

Close to the centre of Netherthong with its narrow streets wandering in all directions, the Clothiers Arms is also the centre of social life in the village. It looks little different today from a picture of 1885, when it carried the same name. Inside, the separate rooms have been opened out into a spacious bar and lounge. From all parts the bar in the corner is in full view, a great help when reordering! And in bad weather it is only a step from the houses opposite to the bar of the Clothiers and company of the Netherthong regulars.

In 1847 Deanhouse Mill was built in the village, using a stream to turn a water wheel for power. Unusually, it dealt with cashmere fleeces, but by 1950 it had closed. Change in the village was very rapid in the twentieth century; at one time there were fourteen shops, but today a post office and a general store have to provide for day-to-day needs.

Netherthong used to be very isolated and self-contained as a hill-top village some 700ft above sea level and served by steep, narrow and winding roads from the

Outside the Clothiers Arms.

Holme valley. This must have produced a way of life that many of the ratepayers wanted to retain, to judge by a public meeting called by the local Chief Constable in February 1866 in response to village opposition to a proposal for a new road to Bridge Mill. The mill buildings occupied both sides of the Huddersfield road in the valley just outside Holmfirth. Of course, in the end change had to come and the new road, steep like the old narrow routes, was built and brought villagers much closer to the wider world.

The strange use of 'thong' at Netherthong, and at its slightly larger neighbours Upperthong and Thongsbridge in the river valley, comes from an early word for a strip of land and from the Danish for a military gathering place. Thong may sound strange, but the people of the village are warm and welcoming, as any visitor to the Clothiers will soon discover.

RICHMOND: *THE BISHOP BLAIZE*

Richmond: A1/A1M to Catterick, then A6136.

Of all the pubs in Yorkshire carrying names connected with the woollen industry, here in the Market Place at Richmond in the twenty-first century is an example few people would recognise. Fortunately a plaque on the wall of the Bishop Blaize in Richmond unveiled in 1992 now records the link with St Blazius, who was adopted as the patron saint of woolcombers.

Martyred in Armenia by the Romans in AD 316, he was tortured and put to death by the use of iron combs to tear his flesh. The similarity of these to the combs used by woolcombers in the early textile industry made him greatly venerated; indeed, some believed him to have invented woolcombing. His emblem has two crossed candles and a comb. Combing is, of course, a preparatory process in the woollen industry.

The Bishop Blaize premises were probably used for wool distribution in Tudor times. In a town such as Richmond there would have been many houses where spinning or weaving was a home industry and the countryside around supplied the fleeces to textile workers. The pub's position on the Market Place would have added to its industrial and commercial importance, but its cultural contribution should also be remembered. In its long room plays were performed by travelling actors in the years before the famous Georgian Theatre was opened in the eighteenth century.

The Bishop Blaize, Richmond.

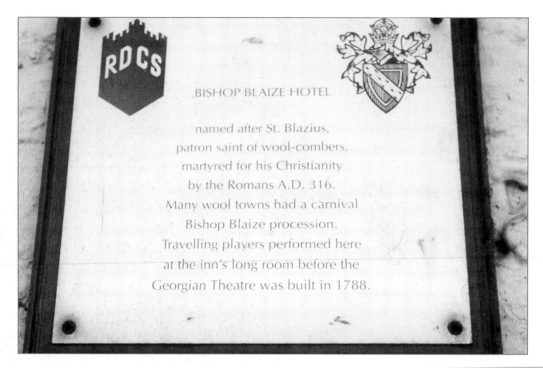

Like other Yorkshire wool towns Richmond would celebrate the Feast of St Blaize on 3 February. In large cities such as Bradford there was an annual dinner and festival with a huge procession of hundreds of workers from all the textile trades including, of course, the woolcombers. Flags and colourful costumes were displayed and bands played.

These activities were at their greatest and finest in the eighteenth and nineteenth centuries just as the factory system had begun to transform the woollen industry. It was mechanisation and the fear of the loss of jobs that brought an end to the festivals that were held every seven years and to the public commemoration of the martyrdom of St Blaize.

TODMORDEN: *WEAVERS ARMS*

Todmorden: M62 J20 to Rochdale, then A58/A6033. Or M65 J10 to Burnley then A646.

By all the rules, the Weavers Arms should not have survived. An old postcard shows the entry to Silent Lane from Burnley Road, Todmorden, partly hidden by shops, including a newsagent's shop on one corner and the Oddfellows Arms on the other. The shops have now gone and the Oddfellows' conversion to apartments has changed the scenery, but the Weavers' landlord believes that Silent Lane is aptly named because you can miss it so easily, as he did on his first visit.

As recently as 1939 there were thirty-three cotton mills and associated businesses in Todmorden; not one mill is operating today. The Weavers' neighbour was once the

The Weavers Arms.

huge Adam Royd Mill owned by Charles Crabtree Ltd, now gone like the rest, its premises occupied by companies producing metal units and electrical equipment. The courtyards of weavers' cottages, tiny houses reached through arches and alleyways that housed many of the pub's customers living opposite were cleared; the area is now a car park.

If the Weavers Arms had been a bigger pub, the loss of three cotton mills in its immediate area would have spelt disaster, but it is a single room establishment with a small bar and one snooker table. It does not need many customers to be crowded and everyone knows everybody else.

An old issue of the Todmorden Official Guide refers to it as a beerhouse and lodging house in 1851. The lodging house notice that once existed on the wall can no longer be seen, neither is there an obvious sign of the accommodation needed for lodgers. An attic window is high up at the Burnley road end of the building, but a row of cottages is built against the opposite gable end. It must have been very dark and extremely cramped when the innkeeper, his family, a servant and the lodgers, thirty-five people, were all at home. But cramped would have perfectly described the nineteenth-century living conditions in the whole area round Silent Lane.

Todmorden is an extraordinary town by any measure, linked by its valley communications to Rochdale and Burnley in Lancashire rather than via the Calder valley to Yorkshire. In fact, until 1888 the town was divided, the boundaries of the counties passing through the Town Hall, where the pediment on the façade has representations of Lancashire industry on the left and those of Yorkshire on the right.

The Freemasons Arms, once a next-door neighbour to the Weavers Arms and now apartments.

The steep valley sides limit Todmorden's sunshine hours and on an overcast day its character as a former mill town is plain to see. In 1829 the Fielden company had the largest weaving shed in the world; the other big cotton families were the Cockcrofts and the Crabtrees. The railways came, of course, and there are two massive stone viaducts at opposite ends of the Burnley road.

Yet industrialists were also benefactors and reformers. John Fielden, MP for Todmorden, who became rich through cotton, worked for improvements in factory conditions and supported the Ten Hour Bill. He is buried at the Unitarian church of 1865 built by his sons in his memory; their fine family home was in Centre Vale Park across the Burnley road from Silent Lane and the Weavers. Both house and park are now open for the benefit of the public.

One of Todmorden's proudest claims is that it is the only town in the world to have had two Nobel prize winners: Sir John Cockcroft in 1951 for his research in the field of nuclear physics and Professor Sir Geoffrey Wilkinson in 1973 for his work in chemistry.

WHITLEY: *THE WOOLPACK INN*

Whitley: M1 J38, A637 to Grangemoor roundabout, then B6118. In Grangemoor village turn at Whitley sign.

Located at the corner of Scopsley Lane in the small village of Whitley south-west of Dewsbury, the pub is just 2 miles from the larger settlement of Thornhill. Both places were typical textile villages in the days of domestic spinning and weaving, but once mills using water power were built in the river valleys, towns like Dewsbury and Huddersfield grew and many workers left villages such as Whitley for work in the towns; others went to work in one of the Thornhill local mines.

Going back over 200 years to the early days of the pub, much wool traffic would have passed by the corner of Scopsley Lane on its way from the Barnsley and Sheffield area to cross the Pennines to the wool markets of Manchester. Horses or mules and their drivers would have been glad to see the pub and be able to halt there for rest and refreshment. Their heavy woolpacks will have given the pub its name, one easily remembered by travellers in general as well as by the regular wool men.

The Woolpack at Whitley, outside and inside.

The Woolpack's beginnings were very modest, as it occupied just one room in a series of back-to-back cottages and remaining this size until 1966, when the property was sold to a local businessman. As and when cottages became vacant, facilities were extended and improved. Successive refurbishments provided a snug, a cocktail bar and a restaurant; most recently fifteen en-suite bedrooms were added.

Today the Woolpack describes itself as 'a pub with atmosphere – and style'. It is good to see that its part in the woollen industry is remembered in the menu with Woolpack Specials and Weavers' Specials.

The handsome pub sign recalls the years when it was the wool men who were pulling up outside; modern travellers may be different, and are glad to have a spacious car park, but the story of the Woolpack is a long and continuing one.

3. YORKSHIRE'S TV PUBS

The importance of the local to its regulars and to the community it serves is not open to challenge; it is the very heart of the locality where news is passed on, protests are born and judgements are made.

So-called TV sitcoms and soaps use the pub scene as a means of introducing the members of the cast and of showing their reactions to developments in a story. We soon learn who can be trusted and admired and those who are dishonest and unpleasant. Before long they appear to viewers to be real people; set against a real pub and countryside that viewers can recognise, the impact is both subtle and profound. Every morning following an episode is an opportunity for viewers to talk through the previous night's happenings and to forecast what will happen next.

Some of the most successful and popular TV series have been set in the Yorkshire landscape and tell tales of Yorkshire folk. The pubs involved have become so famous that they are now visitor attractions for that reason alone; their TV role has created for them an entitlement to be considered historic pubs of Yorkshire.

Some of the cast of *Last of the Summer Wine*, with Ron, former landlord of the White Horse.

ASKRIGG: *KING'S ARMS HOTEL*

Askrigg: A1M and A1 to Leeming Bar then A684 west via Leyburn. At Bainbridge turn right; Askrigg c. 1 mile.

John Pratt's love of horses was to have important consequences for Askrigg. Born locally, he appears to have inherited wealth from his father who was in the coaching business in London. While a student at Cambridge and afterwards he decided to build stables, known as Lodge Yard, in 1752. In front of the stables was a hound pit, where as Master of the Askrigg Harriers he kept the pack of hounds.

On the main street Pratt continued to build: the King's Arms that dates from the 1760s and the neighbouring handsome Manor House, his own home.

Eighteenth-century Askrigg was a wealthy village and had been for centuries, with a number of small-scale industries, including clock making, brewing and woollen knitting using fleeces from Wensleydale sheep. It had a market charter dating from Elizabethan times; the market cross with its five steps stands next to St Oswald's Church, only a few yards away from the King's Arms. Before the turnpike was built on the opposite side of the river Ure the road through Askrigg was used for through traffic, including the coach between Richmond and Lancaster which called at the King's Arms. As the importance of Hawes grew so Askrigg's prosperity declined; but the coming of the railway brought a return to its former business activity.

Above: Askrigg village.
Opposite: The King's Arms Hotel at Askrigg.

One fireplace at the King's Arms . . .

. . . and a second fireplace in the parlour.

In about 1800, some years after John Pratt's death, the ownership of the King's Arms passed to Joseph Lodge who extended the premises. He built the Assembly Rooms that served as a meeting place for the Askrigg Equitable, Benevolent and Friendly Society founded by Lodge to protect members from poverty arising from sickness and accident. The society is still in existence and continues to meet at the King's Arms. Lodge's social conscience was matched by his business acumen, and he set up a brewery behind the King's Arms and supplied other innkeepers. The brewery seems to have been working for some fifty years.

A number of changes and events took place in the twentieth century, perhaps the most remarkable being the use of the King's Arms as the Drovers Inn in the TV series *All Creatures Great and Small*, and Askrigg being selected to represent Darrowby, where James Herriot, Siegfried and Tristan were based. The three rooms used for *All Creatures Great and Small* were a providential discovery. The producer's verdict can only have been 'look no further'. Certainly they were better than any studio set. The bar, which was once a tack room, has its original massive fireplace and a wide range of riding gear, while the other two rooms at front and rear were a restaurant and small bar. The bar is so familiar that it would not be surprising to see James and Tristan arriving for a drink.

Even more recent has been a complete redevelopment of the rear buildings of the pub and Lodge Yard. Together with new buildings, a complete transformation has taken place. Through an archway a charming house, the Dovecot, can be seen on the site of the old brewery. The old stable range has been totally converted into apartments; facing the stables is the hound pit, now an attractive garden.

It is over 250 years since John Pratt started a chain of unlikely events that have continued with the opening of the 'new' Lodge Yard in 1999. One can be confident that the changes already made will not be the last.

ESHOLT: *THE WOOLPACK*

Esholt: A6037 from Bradford to Shipley, then turn right A6038. In about 1½ miles turn right for Esholt.

This pub became famous in *Emmerdale*, which began its long TV series (as *Emmerdale Farm*) in 1972. It was 1976 when a new Beckindale was needed and Esholt became a film village. At that time the pub's name was the Commercial, but a countryside name was thought to be more appropriate, hence the Woolpack, which it has retained.

The Woolpack at Esholt.

Only the exterior of the pub and scenes in the village were ever filmed, so there are no recollections of the bar seen on television. Because the number of weekly episodes of *Emmerdale* was increased it became essential to build a film set of the interior away from the TV studios; this is located on part of the Harewood House estate near Leeds.

In spite of the Woolpack's brief life as a piece of scenery it became much loved, as did Esholt, which is one of the stops on TV 'Soaps Tours'. Coach parties from distant parts such as Cornwall and Sunderland, even from overseas, are regular visitors; the record for the Woolpack was thirty-two coaches in a single day, and of course large numbers of cars bring additional *Emmerdale* fans. Needless to say, there is a large car park.

Although Esholt today is just a residential village on the outskirts of Shipley and Bradford, it had an industrial past. In the nineteenth century most of the villagers were factory workers employed in the two mills at Esholt, one a woollen mill and the other specialising in the production of worsted. No doubt even earlier there was handloom weaving in the cottages near the pub and the church. Those handloom weavers would be astonished that their village had become familiar to millions of people today.

GOATHLAND: *THE GOATHLAND HOTEL* (THE TV AIDENSFIELD ARMS)

Goathland: A64 York to Malton, then left on A169 to Pickering. At Pickering continue on A169 Whitby road. After Saltersgate fork left for Goathland.

Such is the power of TV that popular series using Yorkshire locations create a huge following anxious to visit the places used as a background to the action week by week. Who knows, filming might be going on, and seeing the actors would be a great bonus.

The filming of *Heartbeat* began at Goathland in 1991 and this series still has over ten million viewers. Based on that figure, a massive number of visitors would be expected to go to the Goathland Hotel and to receive the reply, 'Yes, we are the Aidensfield Arms'. Of course, the question is obvious, and it was not difficult for the management to analyse the questions that staff were asked most frequently. The result was a leaflet, 'Heartbeat: Questions Answered', which was put on sale at the hotel, its proceeds going to charity. In the first two weeks 380 copies were sold – answering visitors' queries, benefiting charity and helping to maintain the sanity of hotel staff.

Perhaps it is necessary to add that filming is still going on, but not inside the hotel; after five years the film makers built a set of the bar at the studio for ease of filming, and as a convenience for staff trying to carry out their normal daily work in the hotel.

Goathland's wonderful setting in the middle of the North York Moors National Park made the village a tourist hot spot many years before *Heartbeat*, with Whitby

The Goathland Hotel.

Above: Inside the Goathland Hotel.
Below left: 'Aidensfield Stores' and *right,* 'Aidensfield Garage'.

and the sea nearby. In addition to the walkers and nature lovers already attracted to the area, the opening of the North York Moors Railway from Pickering to Grosmont with a station at Goathland brought even more tourists.

Of the early days of the Goathland Hotel we know that it was built for a Mr Smailes, who owned the Pier Hotel at Whitby; its licence came as a transfer from the Hare and Hounds, a beer house that was accompanied by 13 acres of land.

The first tenants were John Hill and his family in 1884; two generations of the Hills held the licence until after the Second World War, having bought the hotel in 1923. In the 1880s opening hours were from 6 a.m. to 10 p.m.; all the drinking water had to be carried in buckets on a yoke from a spring below Goathland station. Life was hard, but little luxuries seem to have been cheap – at today's prices: beer was 1½d a glass, gin 2d a tot and tobacco 3d per ounce.

At that time the Goathland Hotel was the local transport provider, with three horses and three carriages that met all trains at the station. A return ticket to Pickering or Whitby would have cost 15s and coal was carted from the station at 6d per half ton.

The stone-built Goathland Hotel of today with its two bay windows, central doorway and tall stone chimneys on the gable ends looks spacious and comfortable. Saloon bar, lounge bar and restaurant provide ample accommodation and there are eight en-suite bedrooms. Go early at busy meal times to avoid having to wait.

No doubt past generations of Goathland villagers were not surprised to see holidaymakers walking in the lovely countryside, staying at the Goathland Hotel and visiting the village shops. In their wildest dreams they could not have imagined the crowded car parks and coaches unloading parties on TV tours. Still less would they be able to understand why the Aidensfield Arms, the Aidensfield Stores and the Garage and Scripps' Funeral Services could become such important parts of people's lives. Why would it be important where the police station is (at a former police station in Otley) or where Gina is today?

Have *you* been to Goathland yet?

JACKSON BRIDGE: *THE WHITE HORSE*

Jackson Bridge: A616 Huddersfield–Sheffield a mile south of New Mill. Fork right down a steep hill.

Everything about Jackson Bridge is steep. Past the White Horse, Scholes Road climbs steeply out of the valley, stone houses with their upper floor windows showing clearly that they were once occupied by handloom weavers. On the opposite side of the mill beck and bridge, houses cling to the hillside; one of these is occupied by a former landlord of the White Horse, Ron Backhouse and his wife Ruth. Had it not been for Ron's enthusiasm and their warm welcome, TV cameras might never have visited Jackson Bridge and the White Horse.

The White Horse at Jackson Bridge.

Standing by the side of the bridge, its garden washed by the beck, is the pub, traditional in style and purpose-built in 1830. Not, of course, ancient by any measure, but loved and much-visited on account of its regular use as a watering hole by the famous three: Foggy, Clegg and Compo in *Last of the Summer Wine*. Close to Holmfirth, the location of Sid's Café and the home of Nora Batty, Ron and Ruth provided just the right atmosphere in the right place for a refreshment stop for the trio on their antics around the countryside. On the hill above the White Horse in a row of stone houses is the TV home of Clegg; next door is the home of Howard and his long-suffering wife Pearl.

The bar and lounge are heavily decorated with hundreds of photographs of the years of filming done here. Ron became a regular member of the cast as the landlord never quite able to bring order out of chaos and often driven to see 'our heroes' off the premises.

The White Horse was always a place for charity fund-raising. The annual auction that followed Harvest Festival there was perhaps less spectacular than some of the ideas to raise money. On Boxing Day 1982 Bernard Fish went over the waterfall behind the pub in a barrel and the next year Ron served five steak dinners to customers in 3ft of water in the dam by the bridge. The most ambitious idea was to go by canoe from Jackson Bridge to the Humber Bridge; even if the early part of the journey had to be on foot owing to lack of water, the participants made it in the end.

The interior of the White Horse as featured in *Last of the Summer Wine*.

It was January 1987 when the first TV outside broadcast for Breakfast TV took place. Where else? At Jackson Bridge, of course – and it was very nearly snowbound.

What existed here 250 years ago? Perhaps only an inconvenient crossing of the beck: certainly not a community as there is today. In 1684, according to the *Huddersfield Examiner*, a Mr Henry Jackson who owned property at Meal Hill east of the Sheffield road built a new hall at Totties between Scholes and Holmfirth on the west side. To make an easier journey from one house to the other he built a bridge over the beck at his own expense; this became known as Jackson's Bridge, later Jackson Bridge, where the village and the White Horse were eventually established.

Behind the bar at the White Horse one of the brass plaques says 'In 1832 on this spot nothing happened'. Perhaps so, but a great deal has happened since.

The Bradford statue (see pages 178–9).

4. YORKSHIRE'S COMMEMORATIVE PUBS

What could be more natural than for a person of the stature of Sir Winston Churchill to be chosen for the name of a pub, especially if he happens to be much respected by the landlord? A number of Sir Winston Churchills are to be found in widely separated parts of the country. There are also many Robin Hoods all over England – including Yorkshire, at Bradford, curiously having no direct connection with the hero of Sherwood Forest.

It is perhaps to reflect their achievements that people of local fame (and sometimes notoriety!) are remembered in pub names as well as in statues and memorials.

The following are some of the best known in Yorkshire, which have created a special interest in the pubs concerned.

The interior of the Richard Oastler showing its preserved gallery and painted ceiling that were original features of the chapel.

BRIGHOUSE: *RICHARD OASTLER*

Brighouse: M62 to J25 then A644 into Brighouse.

Here is a pub with a remarkable history and commemorating a remarkable man. In fact it is the only name it ever had – as a pub – because until 1983 it was the Park Chapel, Bethel Street; as such it will be known and remembered by many people in Brighouse. That name came from its foundation as a Wesleyan chapel in Brighouse Park in 1795.

A new chapel building in Bethel Street (originally Brighouse Lane) was opened in June 1878, having cost £10,000 including the organ and furnishings. There had been disagreements within the Wesleyan congregation and the new chapel came to be used by the Methodists; they decided in 1983 to close it as a place of worship, and then came its first change of use – into an indoor market. But it was not as a market that the chapel's future lay: it was as a pub.

Taken over by the J.D. Wetherspoon organisation, it was converted into the Richard Oastler and opened on 23 November 1999. The conversion was a painstaking project, handled by architects Tuffins of Guildford, retaining the organ and gallery and providing a large ground floor area for dining and drinking; the curved bar is pleasantly located below the gallery.

The Richard Oastler, Brighouse.

One of the most surprising and successful decisions was to retain the coloured ceiling; the style of painting has been described as that of Tiepolo, the notable Italian artist. One of his great works, *Assumption*, is at Ascott, the National Trust house in Buckinghamshire.

But why Richard Oastler? Like many Wetherspoon pubs, the Richard Oastler was named after a local historical figure. Oastler lived for some twenty years at nearby Fixby Hall as steward of the Savile family. He became known as the 'Factory King' for his opposition to child labour and excessive working hours. His letter in 1830 on 'Yorkshire slavery' provoked an outcry when it was published in the *Leeds Mercury*.

In less than three years Parliament had prohibited the employment of children under nine in textile mills and laid down a maximum working day of nine hours for those under thirteen. His campaign for a ten-hour day for adults led to his imprisonment for debt, following which a meeting was called at Brighouse to raise a fund to release him from prison. A famous statue of Oastler which stands in Bradford resulted from that meeting.

When the Ten Hours Bill was passed in 1847 he retired from public life.

CARLTON MINIOTT: *BUSBY STOOP*

Carlton Miniott: A1 to A61 towards Thirsk; pub in 4 miles.

Of all the unusual pub names in Yorkshire, this is one of the strangest, yet to the passer-by there is nothing to explain it. Even the pub sign is a puzzle: a high-backed country-style armchair.

Looking as normal as any attractive country pub and standing traditionally at a busy crossroads, it is an unlikely example of a haunted house. Yet there have been numbers of grisly sightings of the ghost of Thomas Busby here, wearing a gruesome hangman's noose round his neck. For close to the inn he was executed by hanging from a post, or stoop.

Thomas Busby was known to be a heavy drinker and not fond of work. When he was not drinking at the pub he was likely to be found sleeping in his chair. It is not surprising that his wife Elizabeth's father disapproved of Busby and of the marriage that was causing her great unhappiness.

The Busby Stoop, Carlton Miniott.

Thirsk Museum.

One day in 1702 Busby returned home to find his father-in-law had arrived and was sitting in his chair prepared for a confrontation. What followed seems to have been an argument about money and Busby's treatment of Elizabeth. Threats were made and Mr Auty returned home, while Busby spent the rest of the evening drinking himself into a violent rage. He broke into the Auty house, attacked and strangled his father-in-law, then hid his body. Elizabeth told the authorities that she had seen her husband bearing the signs of a struggle, and he was convicted of Mr Auty's murder.

On his arrest Busby was found sitting in his high-backed chair, and was said to have put a curse on anyone who sat in it. Because of the curse and the haunting successive landlords of the pub reserved Busby's chair 'for his use'. From time to time the challenge of the curse proved too much and others used it. Fatal accidents suffered by several of them convinced one landlord that the pub would be better off without Busby's chair, which is now in the Thirsk Museum. Wisely it is exhibited hanging on a wall where it cannot be used as a seat. Ask for the kitchen, where the chair is high up in the corner surrounded by displays of kitchen items from the past.

Thirsk Museum, which is at 16 Kirkgate, is well worth a visit for its exhibits as a whole; the building was the birthplace of Thomas Lord, who was commissioned to find a suitable ground for the White Conduit Club in London. After two moves the club settled at St John's Wood, where the Marylebone Cricket Club still has its home at Lord's.

KNARESBOROUGH: *MOTHER SHIPTON INN*

Low Bridge, Knaresborough: A1M to J47, then A59 west. Three alternative right turns to Knaresborough. Direct route to Mother Shipton is last of these.

Entire books have been written about Mother Shipton – certainly a real life character, probably with a gift of prophecy. She was born in 1488, and the pub that took her name dates back to 1645, so this is a very worthy example of a historic Yorkshire pub.

Located by the Low Bridge crossing of the river Nidd on entering Knaresborough, the pub is additionally well placed in having Mother Shipton's Cave, a famous tourist attraction, immediately behind it. For centuries visitors had to pass through the

MOTHER SHIPTON INN

IN EVERY TOWN THE INN OR TAVERN
HAS A LONG HISTORY & THE NAMES
OF OUR PUBLIC HOUSES HAVE A
DIVERSITY OF HISTORICAL VALUE &
ORIGIN.

THE "MOTHER SHIPTON" WAS NAMED
AFTER ENGLANDS MOST FAMOUS
PROPRIETRESS. MOTHER SHIPTON WAS
BORN IN 1488 IN HER FAMOUS CAVE
AT KNARESBOROUGH & FOR MORE
THAN 500 YEARS HER WORD HAS BEEN
RESPECTED AND FEARED.

SOME PROPHECIES HAVE BEEN FULFILLED
& OTHERS REMAIN TO BE SEEN!

"CARRIAGES WITHOUT HORSES SHALL GO
& ACCIDENTS FILL THE WORLD WITH WOE"

"AROUND THE WORLD THOUGHT SHALL FLY
IN THE TWINKLING OF AN EYE"

"THE WORLD SHALL END WHEN THE HIGH
BRIDGE IS THRICE FALLEN"

THE "MOTHER SHIPTON" PUBLIC HOUSE
STANDS BESIDE THE SAID BRIDGE WHICH
HAS FALLEN TWICE ALREADY.

pub to visit the cave and sign the visitors' book, which includes the name of Queen Anne and other people of historical importance.

Today the pub has a main bar area, the Oak Room, a family room, a non-smoking room and a spacious beer garden overlooking the river with a good view of the bridge. There are plenty of historical items around as a reminder that the pub goes back a very long way. In the window facing the bar is the famous Guy Fawkes table from Scotton Old Hall between Knaresborough and Ripon, where he lived for a while. Look for the metal plate on the top giving details.

Many pubs are described as having 'atmosphere'. Here at Mother Shipton there is much, much more; one clue is the request for games to be played nicely in the family room because Peggy, the

The Mother Shipton Inn, Knaresborough.

The games room at the Mother Shipton.

resident ghost, does not like unruly children. Once, many years ago, Peggy, a gypsy lady on her way to the Appleby Horse Fair, an ancient gypsy gathering, quarrelled with her husband, who stabbed her with a broken glass. She was dragged through the games room and her body disposed of somewhere outside, but it is at the Mother Shipton where the ever-forgiving Peggy waits for her husband to return.

She taps the licensee on the shoulder and tells her how sad and lonely she is. This is always during the second week in June when the Appleby Horse Fair is held; broken glass behind the bar signals Peggy's activities. Although Peggy has good relations with the licensee, Alkie the pub dog is uneasy at Appleby Horse Fair time, particularly in the games room.

There are other parts of the pub, including the Oak Room, where people have 'feelings'; others where unexplained happenings take place, like the closing of a door upstairs. At one time the so-called Laughing Cavalier used to be heard climbing upstairs, then closing a door. Alterations to the position of the stairs must have baffled him, but he still closes the door!

The pub sign shows Mother Shipton with her stick, hand raised to command attention. Apart from a clinging black cat there is no suggestion of witchcraft, although she was alleged to be a witch in the days when she was said to foretell disasters such as the destruction by flood of the Ouse Bridge in York. No doubt a number of her possible prophecies were attributed to her after the event had taken place, but once her strange talents had been believed her reputation grew. It is perhaps natural that her birthplace should have been linked with the Dropping Well behind the pub; its petrifying water must have mystified people until fairly modern times.

Up and down the country claims have been made as to her birthplace; this might well have been close to the pub in one of the cottages that stood near the Low Bridge. Far less likely is it to have been by the Dropping Well in what is known as Mother Shipton's Cave. Tradition is responsible for what many people believe about King Arthur: this is probably the case with Mother Shipton too. Feel the power of tradition, whatever you believe, by visiting the Mother Shipton Inn and, just behind it, the Dropping Well and the Cave.

LINTON IN CRAVEN: *FOUNTAINE INN*

Linton in Craven: from Skipton B6265, fork right after Cracoe.

Yes – the spelling is right! Dating from the seventeenth century, the white-walled inn was originally three cottages standing on the upper edge of the village green that slopes down to Linton Beck. Its near neighbour, huge in comparison, is the Fountaine Hospital endowed by Richard Fountaine in 1721 and from whom the pub takes its name. Built in the classical style, the hospital, incorporating almshouses and a chapel, may well have been designed by Sir John Vanbrugh.

The Fountaine Inn, Linton.

Linton Hospital.

The pub's tiny bar on the left of the entrance and the snug on the right look out on to the green where ducks from the beck loiter expectantly for food. Their number and appearance speak well for the Fountaine's catering, available to the public in a restaurant as well as in the snug. Tradition here is that of low beams, settles and a powerful open fire which attract regulars and visitors alike. Such a fire at their backs for playing the very old pub game Ring the Bull must make for one of the warmest competitions in Yorkshire. Arriving at the snug as the ring seeks out the bull makes swift avoiding action wise.

Pub games go back a very long way: dominoes, draughts, darts and pool are played nationwide, also skittles and bowls where there is space for a green; while others have a local flavour. Ring the Bull is one of these, with what are best described as 'flexible' rules, while Knur and Spell is a curious Yorkshire phenomenon that requires competitors to hit a small ball with a stick as far as possible – outdoors, naturally (see pages 112–13).

Stepping out of the Fountaine's door is a revelation. The green, with its monument recording Linton's win in the Loveliest Village in the North competition in 1949, lies above the shining beck and its five crossings: ford, stepping stones, packhorse bridge, clapper bridge and road bridge are the alternatives. Beyond, stone-built cottages clustered closely together are the heart and history of the village. One belonging to the Proctor family has their initials and the date 1639 above the ancient doorway.

Snowdrops at Linton.

But the village is by no means only a cottage community. By the road bridge is the seventeenth-century White Abbey, once the home of the novelist Halliwell Sutcliffe who wrote about the Dales; the garden has a small gate allowing private entry from the stepping stones across the beck. On the opposite side from here is Georgian Linton House and close by is the Old Hall, seventeenth century with a prominent porch and gable curved in the Dutch style. So much, as they say, in little compass.

The Fountaine Inn and Linton are, like a first visit to Venice, a memory to treasure. Anyone going to the pub and the village at snowdrop time will find it an unforgettable experience.

STAITHES: *CAPTAIN COOK INN*

Staithes: A1M to J49, fork right A168 Teeside direction. At Thirsk continue north A19. In 11 miles fork right A172. At Stokesley fork right A173 then A174.

Of all the great men of Yorkshire to expect to find on a pub sign, the name of Captain Cook must surely be the most likely. After all, the great navigator was born at Marton near Middlesbrough, spent his schooldays at Great Ayton, where the school is now a small museum, and then went to Staithes as an apprentice to a shopkeeper.

It is at Staithes that the Captain Cook Inn can be found and – surprisingly – nowhere else. Equally surprising is the fact that the pub's life began as the Station Hotel in 1883 to provide for passengers on the ill-fated Middlesbrough to Whitby line. Such was the delay in completing the line serving Staithes that the aims of the railway were never fulfilled.

The line was intended to transport fish, but the fishermen of Staithes were never able to compete with the fleets at ports like Hull and Grimsby, especially at a time of declining fish stocks. A second

aim was to bring in holidaymakers from the north, only for the decline of industry and employment in the Middlesbrough area and the West Riding to ruin that possibility. Staithes station was considered by many as a white elephant and the line was eventually closed in 1958.

No longer was the Station Hotel needed for its original purpose, but the landlord decided, on his retirement, having been a naval convoy man in the Second World War, to rename the pub the Captain Cook Inn. It stands on the access road to the old village and harbour from the A174 Whitby–Saltburn road, so has all the passing traffic. Since there is no parking down the hill at the harbour, a large public car park only a few yards from the pub is a great advantage.

A lounge and games room look out over the road, with a dining room at the rear, where residents and casual diners have meals. The bar is a central feature, while there is a splendid display of beer labels near the door. An outside view confirms the general appearance of a Station Hotel, but the building is attractively decorated and very much looks the part of a comfortable Victorian family home.

When he was sixteen James Cook started work at Staithes: the shop no longer exists, having been swept away by the sea in a violent storm. Many years earlier during his apprenticeship the young man was apparently so fascinated by the atmosphere and activity at Staithes harbour that he decided to go to Whitby to seek a career at sea.

There are several accounts of James Cook's leaving his employer at Staithes, William Sanderson, the most intriguing concerning a missing shilling. This version is about a shiny new shilling that Mr Sanderson knew had been paid in, but was

Captain Cook Inn, Staithes.

The bar at the Captain Cook.

Staithes harbour.

missing later; the explanation for this was said to be Cook's wish to collect the new coin, replacing it with an old one of his own.

James Cook's future as a great navigator and discoverer was enough to make him a Yorkshire hero; no wonder that Staithes people cherish his early years as one of them. His portrait hangs proudly outside the pub as evidence of their regard for him and his achievements.

STOKESLEY: *THE WHITE SWAN AND THE CAPTAIN COOK BREWERY*

Stokesley: A1M to J49, take A168 Teeside direction. At Thirsk continue north A19. In 11 miles fork right A172.

Although the Captain Cook Inn at Staithes is the sole known pub in Yorkshire carrying his name, here at Stokesley there is an attractive small brewery with his name; after all, Cook's early life was spent at Marton and Great Ayton, both in the vicinity of Stokesley.

The White Swan is an early eighteenth-century coaching inn at Stokesley's West End, a particularly pleasant area with fine houses. Its arch on the right-hand side of the front leads to its courtyard where coaching activities would have taken place. Today the stable block has been converted into the Captain Cook Brewery, which began business on 1 November 2000.

Two fermentation vessels inside the little brewery. It is a four-barrel plant operated by Head Brewer David Ward. Output is four barrels in an eight-hour working.

The White Swan.

Beers brewed here, Slipway (the first), Sunset and Navigator, all carry the memory of James Cook. A dark winter brew, Black Porter has also proved popular. These are traditionally brewed beers and virtually all the output is sold through the White Swan.

The pub is beautifully maintained both outside and in. It is small with just one bar, but has that quality of presenting itself warmly and well. Anyone interested in Captain Cook and brewing can make arrangements with the licensee of the White Swan to visit the brewery.

Acknowledgements

I am deeply indebted to many people and organisations for their help in collecting material and taking photographs for this book. Busy licensees found time to provide information or to point a finger in the right direction and have allowed me freedom to wander with my camera.

I acknowledge with gratitude the help given by breweries and pub companies. The support of CAMRA and the reports and recommendations of Yorkshire CAMRA branches have been invaluable. Societies and organisations that have been of great assistance are the Brontë Society, the Pennine Line Partnership, the Pork Pie Appreciation Society, the Sowerby Bridge Rush Bearing Association, the Towton Battlefield Society and North Kirklees Youth Action.

I particularly wish to acknowledge local sources of information in Hull. CAMRA Hull and East Yorkshire Branch through their Chairman Alan Canvess not only shortlisted a number of pubs for consideration but also provided a guided tour. Detailed research work into all aspects of the history of the two Hull pubs has been done by the Local History Unit at Hull College and compiled by Robert Barnard. The Hull Civic Society has also done valuable work in this field and without references from their respective papers much of interest and significance would have gone unrecorded here.

Among the many contacts and friends whose researches have been of the utmost help are Barry Everett (Heath), David Green (Huddersfield), Mark Reid (North Yorkshire), Chris Heath (Denby Dale), Jason Boom (Luddenden), Rod Kaye (Wakefield), Ron Backhouse (Jackson Bridge and host of *Summer Wine*), Derek Woodhouse (Roberttown), John Howard (Scarborough and Staithes), Barrie Pepper (Leeds and Yorkshire pubs), Claire Wilkinson (Ribblehead), the Truelove family (Three Acres), Bill Williams (Harrogate), Tony Brookes (Head of Steam Ltd), John and Nancy Teal (Roydhouse), Ralph and Sarah Whitelock and Cathy Turfrey (Whitelocks), and Christian Horton (Samuel Smith).

Local authority services have been readily and generously offered: Bradford and Keighley Libraries, Calderdale Libraries, Museums and Arts Service, Kirklees Libraries and Information Service, North Yorkshire County Council Library and Information Service, Hull Tourism and Huddersfield Tolson Memorial Museum.

Books, periodicals and guides consulted have been numerous. These include *Historic Inns of England* (Ted Bruning), *British Inn Signs* (Eric R. Delderfield), *York's Historic Inns* (Pete Coxon), *Denby & District* (Chris Heath), *Town Trails: North Yorkshire* (Mark Reid), *The Beverley Arms* (John Markham), *Huddersfield Examiner*, *Halifax Evening Courier*, *Yorkshire Post* and *York & County Press*.

Any errors or omissions in the book are entirely my responsibility. To anyone who gave help in any way with the research and is not mentioned above I offer my grateful thanks and most sincere apologies.